I0010282

Raspberry Pi Zero W Wireless Projects

Go mobile with the world's most popular microprocessor

Vasilis Tzivaras

BIRMINGHAM - MUMBAI

Raspberry Pi Zero W Wireless Projects

Copyright © 2017 Packt Publishing

All rights reserved. No part of this book may be reproduced, stored in a retrieval system, or transmitted in any form or by any means, without the prior written permission of the publisher, except in the case of brief quotations embedded in critical articles or reviews.

Every effort has been made in the preparation of this book to ensure the accuracy of the information presented. However, the information contained in this book is sold without warranty, either express or implied. Neither the author, nor Packt Publishing, and its dealers and distributors will be held liable for any damages caused or alleged to be caused directly or indirectly by this book.

Packt Publishing has endeavored to provide trademark information about all of the companies and products mentioned in this book by the appropriate use of capitals. However, Packt Publishing cannot guarantee the accuracy of this information.

First published: August 2017

Production reference: 1230817

Published by Packt Publishing Ltd.
Livery Place
35 Livery Street
Birmingham
B3 2PB, UK.
ISBN 978-1-78829-052-4

www.packtpub.com

Credits

Author
Vasilis Tzivaras

Reviewer
Taifoun Sianko

Commissioning Editor
Vijin Boricha

Acquisition Editor
Prachi Bisht

Content Development Editor
Eisha Dsouza

Technical Editor
Naveenkumar Jain

Copy Editors
Ulka Manjrekar
Laxmi Subramanian

Project Coordinator
Kinjal Bari

Proofreader
Safis Editing

Indexer
Rekha Nair

Graphic
Kirk D'Penha

Production Coordinator
Shantanu Zagade

About the Author

Vasilis Tzivaras is a computer science engineer who lives in Greece. He is the author of the *Building a Quadcopter with Arduino* and is also the chair of the IEEE University of Ioannina Student Branch. He is currently working on projects relevant to robotics, home automation, and smart security systems. He is also an enthusiast about Internet of Things technology and drones.

About the Reviewer

Taifoun Sianko is a computer science graduate from university of Ioannina. He just started his career as software developer. During his study, he has been studied data structures, compilers and algorithms. His love for development and mobiles pushed him to begin Android development and UI design as freelancer. He also makes his own automation based on Arduino and Raspberry Pi.

www.PacktPub.com

For support files and downloads related to your book, please visit www.PacktPub.com. Did you know that Packt offers eBook versions of every book published, with PDF and ePub files available? You can upgrade to the eBook version at www.PacktPub.com and as a print book customer, you are entitled to a discount on the eBook copy. Get in touch with us at service@packtpub.com for more details. At www.PacktPub.com, you can also read a collection of free technical articles, sign up for a range of free newsletters and receive exclusive discounts and offers on Packt books and eBooks.

https://www.packtpub.com/mapt

Get the most in-demand software skills with Mapt. Mapt gives you full access to all Packt books and video courses, as well as industry-leading tools to help you plan your personal development and advance your career.

Why subscribe?

- Fully searchable across every book published by Packt
- Copy and paste, print, and bookmark content
- On demand and accessible via a web browser

Customer Feedback

Thanks for purchasing this Packt book. At Packt, quality is at the heart of our editorial process. To help us improve, please leave us an honest review on this book's Amazon page at `https://www.amazon.com/dp/1788290526`.

If you'd like to join our team of regular reviewers, you can e-mail us at `customerreviews@packtpub.com`. We award our regular reviewers with free eBooks and videos in exchange for their valuable feedback. Help us be relentless in improving our products!

Table of Contents

Preface 1

Chapter 1: Introduction to Raspberry Pi Zero W 7

The Raspberry Pi family 7
Raspberry Pi Zero W 12
Specifications 13
Camera support 16
Accessories 16
    An OTG cable 17
    PowerHub 18
    A GPIO header 19
    MicroSD card and card adapter 20
    An HDMI to mini HDMI cable 20
    An HDMI to VGA cable 21
    RCA jacks 22
A Raspberry Pi Zero W case 22
Distributions 23
    The NOOBS distribution 24
    The Raspbian distribution 25
Distributors 27
Common Issues 28
    Debugging steps 28
    MicroSD card issue 29
    Case protection 29
Summary 29

Chapter 2: IoT and Networking 31

Internet of Things 31
Basic communication protocols 32
    Internet protocols 33
    IoT Protocols 33
        Bluetooth 34
        Zigbee 34
        Z-Wave 34
        6LowPAN 35
        NFC 35
        Wi-Fi 35

LoRaWAN   35
Connecting your Pi   36
  Pi Zero W setup   36
  The internet   36
  Local network   37
  Port forwarding   39
  Connecting to the internet   39
  Networking administration   40
  Connect for command execution   41
  Automatic authentication   42
Connecting for file transfer   43
  FileZilla   43
  SCP   45
Secure the Raspberry Pi and remove others   45
  Firewall   46
Summary   47

Chapter 3: Chatbot   49

User input   49
  Server installation   50
  The chatbot development   54
Chat services   57
  Chatfuel   57
  Frow XO   58
  Converse   58
  Facebook messenger   59
  Google cleverbot   60
Secure data transfer   61
Summary   61

Chapter 4: Mobile Robot   63

Fundamentals of robotics   63
  DC motors   65
  Torque   66
  Wheel   67
  Encoders   68
Hardware overview   70
  DC motor and wheels   73
  Encoder   74
  Arduino microcontroller   75

Motorshield	77
Servo	78
Ultrasonic sensor	79
Bluetooth	82
Breadboard	84
Battery	85
Other components	86
Motor soldering	86
Programming the controller	88
Basic concept	89
Controller development	89
Future ideas	92
Four motor mobile robots	93
Summary	97
Chapter 5: Home Bot	99
Introduction to home bots	99
Socket programming	100
Simple client-server communication	101
Simple server	102
Simple client	105
Advanced client-server communication	107
Advanced server	107
Advanced client	112
Home automation	113
Summary	116
Chapter 6: Security Camera	117
Installing a camera	117
Installing MotionPie	120
Set up multiple network cameras	121
Connecting a camera outside of your local network	121
Configuring MotionPie settings	122
General settings	123
Wireless network	124
Video device	124
File storage	126
Text Overlay	126
Video Streaming	126
Still images	128
Motion Detection	128

Motion Movies   128
Motion Notifications   129
Working Schedule   129
Installing OpenCV   130
Face recognition   131
Summary   136

Chapter 7: Portable Speakers   137

Market speakers   137
Software setup   139
Networking   141
MusicBox   141
Audio   142
Music files   142
Online music services   143
Security   143
Sound players   143
Alsamixer   144
Connect your speaker   145
Music on Pi   146
Mood selection   148
Hardware   149
Code   150
Summary   151

Chapter 8: WebPi Hosting   153

Web hosting   153
Definition   153
Hosting services   155
Domain name   156
DNS   157
Setup   157
Client-server communication   158
Client request   158
Communication protocols   159
Server response   160
Proxy servers and caching   161
Website development   162
XAMPP/LAMPP   163
Accessing the website   164

Remote control   164
  SSH   165
    SSH clients   165
      Windows   165
      Linux   169
    Automating the SSH procedure   170
  SFTP   171
    FileZilla   172
    Terminal   173
Networking   174
  Router access   175
    Port forwarding   176
    Home IP address   177
    Security layers   178
  Security   179
    Router Interface   179
    Computer   181
    ISP   181
  Summary   181
Chapter 9: AlexaPi   183
  Creating an Amazon Developer account   183
  Setting up Raspberry Pi   191
  Installing Alexa   192
  Voice recognition   193
  Official Alexa vs AlexaPi   194
  Network administration   195
  Summary   201
Chapter 10: WeatherPi   203
  The Sense HAT module   203
  Weather station   205
  Initial State   212
  Startup   217
  Summary   220
Index   221

Preface

The new member of the Raspberry Pi family is equipped with wireless and Bluetooth extensions. Through this book you can learn and create awesome projects that allows you to explore the capabilities of the new board. With only $10 you can develop skills and be part of a new world where you can develop your robots, your home automation systems, increase your security layers in your home and much more.

What this book covers

Chapter 1, *Introduction to Raspberry Pi Zero W*, will introduce the new board with the wireless extension. We will mention some modules that you can buy with and give a general overview of the new board.

Chapter 2, *IoT and Networking*, will talk about Internet of Things. Raspberry Pi Zero W is very small, which makes it a perfect board for IoT projects. It is also equipped with **Bluetooth Low Energy** (**BLE**), which minimizes the energy consumption. Lastly, we will give an introduction to networking and how you will interact with the board.

Chapter 3, *Chatbot*, will develop a chatbot. Chatbots are ubiquitous nowadays and usually consist of a client and a server. So we will start by creating a client and then end the chapter by implementing the server side. We will also mention some protocols that chatbots use.

Chapter 4, *Mobile Robot*, will be devoted to robotics. You will learn how to build a two-wheeled mobile robot, and through the chapter you will learn the fundamentals of robotics that are necessary skills for developing any kind of robot.

Chapter 5, *Home Bot*, explains how to build a home bot and automate your home with commands from a local website or your mobile phone. A general system of home automation will be implemented and described.

Chapter 6, *Security Camera*, will demonstrate the implementation of a security system. Adding a camera to your home makes it smarter, and you can always see and record what is going on.

Chapter 7, *Portable Speakers*, chapter is about music. Since the Raspberry Pi Zero W is quite small, it is pretty easy to make it portable and add some speakers to listen to your favorite music wherever you want. You only need a powerbank and you can get your music with you.

Chapter 8, *WebPi Hosting*, is about web hosting and developing. With the Raspberry Pi Zero W board you can host websites and develop simple sites to help you control your home and automate things. Through this chapter you will learn how to make a website, upload it to the Raspberry Pi, and publish it to the world.

Chapter 9, *AlexaPi*, is about the **Alexa Voice Service** (**AVS**) from Amazon. We will upload the AVS to our Raspberry Pi Zero W board and develop a system that allows us to control anything that is connected to the AVS. We can also, talk with Alexa and get answers in questions such as *What time is it?*

Chapter 10, *WeatherPi*, will develop a weathering station with which you can monitor your home or any place you want and get measurements of the temperature and the humidity of the place.

What you need for this book

Even if it works in all operating systems, it is better to have a Linux operating system. You obviously need your basic Raspberry Pi Zero W kit with a camera. Furthermore, you need the SenseHAT module and a microphone or a headset. You also need Bluetooth speaker, and lastly, all the components necessary for the two-wheeled mobile robot.

Who this book is for

If you are a hobbyist or an enthusiast who wants to get their hands on the latest Raspberry Pi Zero W and leverage it to build exciting wireless projects then, this book is for you. Prior programming knowledge with some experience in electronics would be useful.

Conventions

In this book, you will find a number of styles of text that distinguish between different kinds of information. Here are some examples of these styles, and an explanation of their meaning.

Code words in text, database table names, folder names, filenames, file extensions, pathnames, dummy URLs, user input, and Twitter handles are shown as follows: "Create a new file named `cpi` and type the following command."

A block of code is set as follows:

```
[226314.048026] usb 4-2: new full-speed USB device number 82
using uhci_hcd [226314.213273] usb 4-2: New USB device found,
idVendor=0a5c, idProduct=2763 [226314.213280] usb 4-2: New USB
device strings: Mfr=1, Product=2, SerialNumber=0
[226314.213284] usb 4-2: Product: BCM2708 Boot
[226314.213] usb 4-2: Manufacturer: Broadcom
```

Any command-line input or output is written as follows:

```
man <linux-command>
```

New terms and **important words** are shown in bold. Words that you see on the screen, in menus or dialog boxes for example, appear in the text like this: "Click on the **Save** button."

Warnings or important notes appear in a box like this.

Tips and tricks appear like this.

Reader feedback

Feedback from our readers is always welcome. Let us know what you think about this book-what you liked or disliked. Reader feedback is important for us as it helps us develop titles that you will really get the most out of. To send us general feedback, simply e-mail feedback@packtpub.com, and mention the book's title in the subject of your message. If there is a topic that you have expertise in and you are interested in either writing or contributing to a book, see our author guide at www.packtpub.com/authors.

Customer support

Now that you are the proud owner of a Packt book, we have a number of things to help you to get the most from your purchase.

Downloading the example code

You can download the example code files for this book from your account at http://www.packtpub.com. If you purchased this book elsewhere, you can visit http://www.packtpub.com/support and register to have the files e-mailed directly to you.

You can download the code files by following these steps:

1. Log in or register to our website using your e-mail address and password.
2. Hover the mouse pointer on the **SUPPORT** tab at the top.
3. Click on **Code Downloads & Errata**.
4. Enter the name of the book in the **Search** box.
5. Select the book for which you're looking to download the code files.
6. Choose from the drop-down menu where you purchased this book from.
7. Click on **Code Download**.

Once the file is downloaded, please make sure that you unzip or extract the folder using the latest version of:

- WinRAR / 7-Zip for Windows
- Zipeg / iZip / UnRarX for Mac
- 7-Zip / PeaZip for Linux

The code bundle for the book is also hosted on GitHub at https://github.com/PacktPublishing/Raspberry-Pi-Zero-W-Wireless-Projects. We also have other code bundles from our rich catalog of books and videos available at https://github.com/PacktPublishing/. Check them out!

Downloading the color images of this book

We also provide you a PDF file that has color images of the screenshots/diagrams used in this book. The color images will help you better understand the changes in the output. You can download this file from: https://www.packtpub.com/sites/default/files/downloads/RaspberryPiZeroWWireless Projects_ColorImages.pdf.

Errata

Although we have taken every care to ensure the accuracy of our content, mistakes do happen. If you find a mistake in one of our books-maybe a mistake in the text or the code-we would be grateful if you could report this to us. By doing so, you can save other readers from frustration and help us improve subsequent versions of this book. If you find any errata, please report them by visiting http://www.packtpub.com/submit-errata, selecting your book, clicking on the **Errata Submission Form** link, and entering the details of your errata. Once your errata are verified, your submission will be accepted and the errata will be uploaded to our website or added to any list of existing errata under the Errata section of that title.

To view the previously submitted errata, go to https://www.packtpub.com/books/content/support and enter the name of the book in the search field. The required information will appear under the**Errata** section.

Piracy

Piracy of copyrighted material on the Internet is an ongoing problem across all media. At Packt, we take the protection of our copyright and licenses very seriously. If you come across any illegal copies of our works in any form on the Internet, please provide us with the location address or website name immediately so that we can pursue a remedy.

Please contact us at copyright@packtpub.com with a link to the suspected pirated material.

We appreciate your help in protecting our authors and our ability to bring you valuable content.

Questions

If you have a problem with any aspect of this book, you can contact us at questions@packtpub.com, and we will do our best to address the problem.

1
Introduction to Raspberry Pi Zero W

Raspberry Pi Zero W is a new product from the Raspberry Pi Zero family. In early 2017, the Raspberry Pi community announced a new board with a wireless extension. It offers wireless functionality and now anyone can develop their own project without cables or other components. Comparing the new board with Raspberry Pi 3 Model B, we can easily see that it is much smaller, with many possibilities for the Internet of Things. However, what is a Raspberry Pi Zero W, and why do you need it? Let's go through the rest of the family and introduce the new board. In this chapter, we will cover the following topics:

- An overview of the Raspberry Pi family
- An introduction to the new Raspberry Pi Zero W
- Distributions
- Distributors
- Common issues

The Raspberry Pi family

As mentioned previously, Raspberry Pi Zero W is a new member of the Raspberry Pi family of boards. Throughout the years, Raspberry Pi has been evolving and has become more user-friendly with endless possibilities. Let's have a look at the rest of the family, so we can understand how the Pi Zero board is different.

Right now, the *heavy* board is named Raspberry Pi 3 Model B. It is the best solution for projects such as face recognition, video tracking, gaming, or anything else that is demanding:

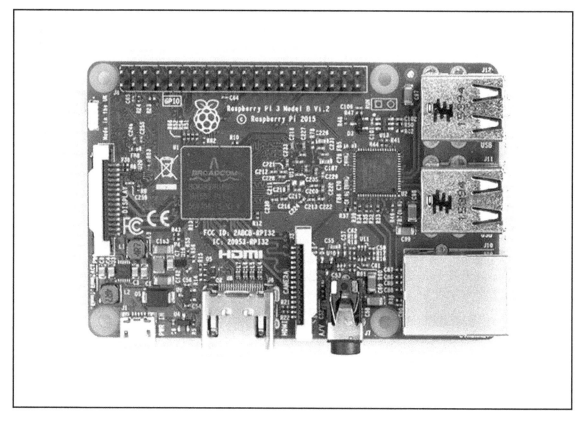

A Raspberry Pi 3 model

This is the third generation of Raspberry Pi boards after Raspberry Pi 2 and has the following specifications:

- A 1.2 GHz 64-bit quad core ARMv8 CPU
- 802.11 n wireless LAN
- Bluetooth 4.1
- Bluetooth Low Energy (BLE)

Like Pi 2, it also has:

- 1 GB RAM
- 4 USB ports
- 40 GPIO pins
- Full HDMI port
- Ethernet port
- Combined 3.5 mm audio jack and composite video
- Camera interface (CSI)
- Display interface (DSI)
- MicroSD card slot (now push-pull rather than push-push)
- VideoCore IV 3D graphics core

The next board is Raspberry Pi Zero, in which Zero W is based, a small, low-cost power board able to do many things:

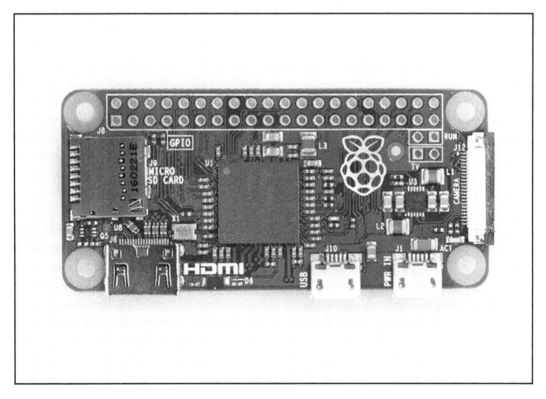

A Raspberry Pi Zero board

The specifications of this board are as follows:

- 1 GHz, single-core CPU
- 512 MB RAM
- Mini HDMI port
- Micro-USB OTG port
- Micro-USB power
- HAT-compatible 40-pin header
- Composite video and reset headers
- CSI camera connector (v1.3 only)

At this point, we should not forget to mention that apart from the boards mentioned previously, there are several other modules and components such as Sense Hat or Raspberry Pi Touch Display available that will work well for advanced projects.

The 7" touchscreen monitor of Raspberry Pi gives users the ability to create all-in-one, integrated projects such as tablets, infotainment systems, and embedded projects:

The Raspberry Pi Touch display

The Sense HAT is an add-on board for Raspberry Pi made especially for the Astro Pi mission. The Sense HAT has an 8×8 RGB LED matrix, a five-button joystick and includes the following sensors:

- Gyroscope
- Accelerometer
- Magnetometer
- Temperature
- Barometric pressure
- Humidity

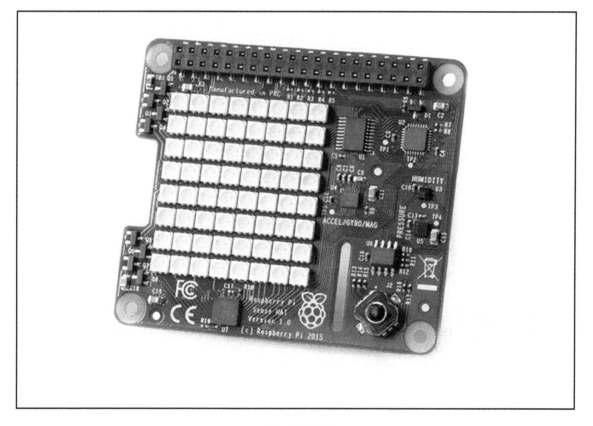

A Sense HAT borad

Stay tuned for new boards and modules at the official website `https://www.raspberrypi.org`.

Raspberry Pi Zero W

Raspberry Pi Zero W is a small device that can be connected to either an external monitor or TV and of course, to the internet. The operating system varies, as there are many distributions on the official page and almost every distribution is based on Linux systems:

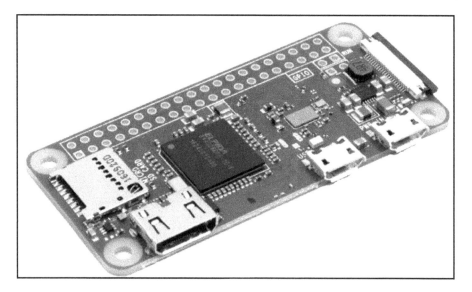

Raspberry Pi Zero W

With Raspberry Pi Zero W, you have the ability to do almost everything from automation to gaming! It is a small computer that allows you to easily program with the help of GPIO pins and some other components such as a camera. Its possibilities are endless! In the next chapter, you will go through some awesome projects with this new board. Since almost all input and output on the Raspberry Pi Zero W board goes through GPIO pins, it is important to keep in mind a pinout diagram. The following is a pinout diagram of the Raspberry Pi Zero W board, which can be handy when soldering buttons or other types of sensors onto your Raspberry Pi board:

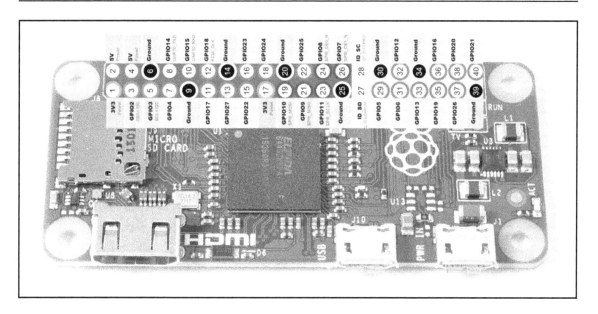

Specifications

If you have bought a Raspberry Pi 3 Model B, you will be familiar with the Cypress CYW43438 wireless chip. It provides 802.11 n wireless LAN and Bluetooth 4.0 connectivity. The new Raspberry Pi Zero W is equipped with this wireless chip as well. The following are the specifications of the new board:

- **Dimensions:** 65 mm × 30 mm × 5 mm
- **SoC:** Broadcom BCM 2835 chip
    - ARM11 at 1 GHz, single-core CPU
    - 512 MB RAM
- **Storage:** MicroSD card
- **Video and Audio:** 1080p HD video and stereo audio via mini HDMI connector
- **Power:** 5V supplied via micro-USB connector
- **Wireless:** 2.4GHz 802.11 n wireless LAN
- **Bluetooth:** Bluetooth classic 4.0 and Bluetooth Low Energy (BLE)
- **Output:** Micro-USB
- **GPIO:** 40-pin GPIO, unpopulated

In the following image, we can see the new Raspberry Pi Zero W equipped with the previously mentioned specifications:

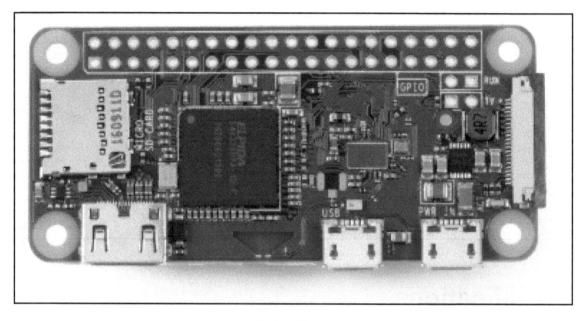

Raspberry Pi Zero W

Notice that all components are at the top of the board, so you can easily choose your case without any problems and keep it safe. As far as the antenna is concerned, it is formed by etching away copper on each layer of the PCB. It may not be visible, as it is in other similar boards, but it works great and offers quite a lot of functionalities:

Raspberry Pi Zero W Capacitors

Also, the product is limited to only one piece per buyer and costs $10. You can buy a full kit with a MicroSD card, a case, and some extra components for about $45, or choose the full kit with a camera that contains a small camera component for $55.

Camera support

Image processing projects, such as video tracking or face recognition, require a camera. In the next image, you can see the official camera support for Raspberry Pi Zero W. The camera can be easily mounted at the side of the board using a cable, similar to the Raspberry Pi 3 Model B board.

The official camera support for Raspberry Pi Zero W

Depending on your distribution, you may need to enable the camera through the command line. More information on the usage of this module will be mentioned in the project chapters.

Accessories

While building projects with the new board, there are some other gadgets that you might find useful to work with. The following is a list of some crucial components. Notice that if you buy a Raspberry Pi Zero W kit, it includes some of them. So, be careful and don't double upon them.

- An OTG cable
- PowerHub
- A GPIO header

- A MicroSD card and card adapter
- An HDMI to mini HDMI cable
- An HDMI to VGA cable

An OTG cable

First of all, an OTG cable is always useful. You can use this cable to power your Raspberry Pi from a power bank or any other power source.

An OTG cable

PowerHub

The second most important component is the PowerHub. A PowerHub is a device powered by a USB or external power source and produces four or more USB ports:

PowerHub

A GPIO header

Next, you might find the GPIO header module handy. Since Raspberry Pi Zero W comes without soldered pins, it is useful to connect GPIO pins over and breadboard:

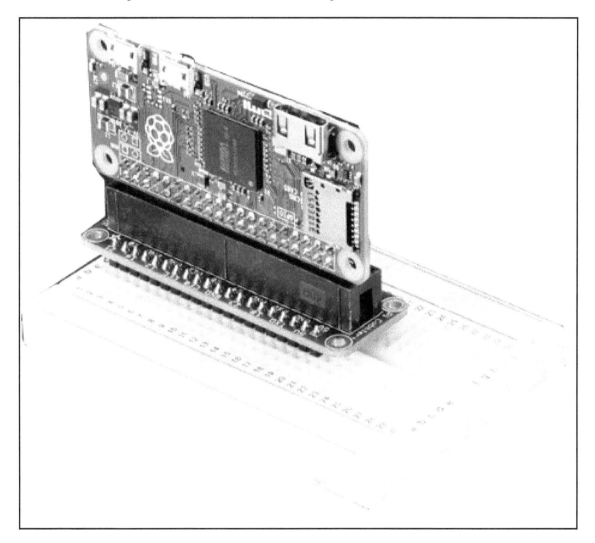

A GPIO header

MicroSD card and card adapter

You might also need a MicroSD card adapter as not every computer has a MicroSD card slot for reading and writing data. It costs quite a few dollars but will save you time.

A MicroSD card and card adapter

An HDMI to mini HDMI cable

Unfortunately, the new Raspberry Pi Zero W does not have a normal HDMI port. It is a bit smaller, and you need the HDMI to mini HDMI cable to expand the port to a normal HDMI. Then, you are free to connect the port with any HDMI-compatible device. So, the next cable is necessary:

An HDMI to mini HDMI cable

An HDMI to VGA cable

Since many monitors are not HDMI compatible, the HDMI to VGA cable allows you to connect the HDMI to mini HDMI cable with an external monitor or TV. When you need to view something on the monitor and it does not support HDMI, this cable is required:

An HDMI to VGA cable

RCA jacks

Lastly, some TVs still use RCA jacks. With this module, you can connect the Pi board to the RCA jack on your TV by simply connecting the two wires, + (signal) and - (ground), of the module.

An RCA jack

A Raspberry Pi Zero W case

Since Raspberry Pi Zero W will be used for various projects, it's good practice to spend some more dollars and buy a case or buy a full kit that comes with the official case, as shown in the next image. The official case is quite protective and exposes only the necessary parts, letting you fully control your board. All the work is done at Kinneir Dufort and T-Zero. The available options are as follows:

- A blank one
- One with an aperture to let you access GPIOs
- One with an aperture and a mounting point for a camera

We can see a Raspberry Pi Zero W case in the following image:

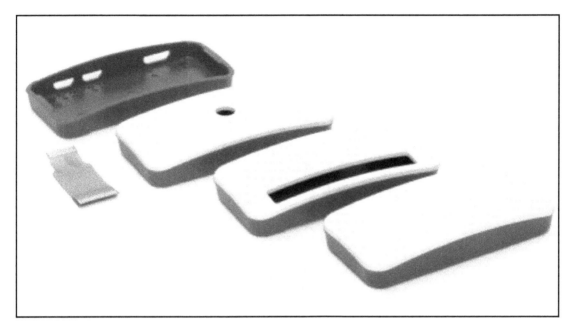

A Raspberry Pi Zero W case

The official case set also includes:

- A short camera adapter, flexi
- A set of rubber feet to make sure that your new Zero W board will not slide off any desk

Distributions

The official site `https://www.raspberrypi.org/downloads/` contains several distributions for downloading. The two basic operating systems that we will analyze later are Raspbian and NOOBS. You can see what the desktop environment looks like in the next image. Both Raspbian and NOOBS allow you to choose from two versions. There is a full version of the operating system and a lite one. Obviously, the lite version does not contain everything that you might use, so if you intend to use your Raspberry with a desktop environment, choose and download the full version.

On the other hand, if you intend to just SSH and do some basic stuff, pick the lite one. It's really up to you, and of course, you can easily download anything you like and rewrite your microSD card.

The NOOBS distribution

Download NOOBS from https://www.raspberrypi.org/downloads/noobs/. The NOOBS distribution is for new users who do not possess much knowledge about Linux systems and Raspberry Pi boards. As the official page says, it is really, "New Out Of Box Software." There are also preinstalled NOOBS SD cards that you can purchase from many retailers, such as Pimoroni, Adafruit, and The Pi Hut, and of course, you can download NOOBS and write your own microSD card. If you are having trouble with a specific distribution, take a look at the following links:

- Full guide: https://www.raspberrypi.org/learning/software-guide/
- View the video: https://www.raspberrypi.org/help/videos/#noobs-setup

The NOOBS operating system contains Raspbian, and it provides various other operating systems available to download.

The Raspbian distribution

Download Raspbian from the official page `https://www.raspberrypi.org/downloads/raspbian/`. Raspbian is the officially supported operating system. It can be installed through NOOBS or by downloading the image file from the following link and going through the guide on the official website.

Image file can be downloaded from: `https://www.raspberrypi.org/documentation/installation/installing-images/README.md`

It has plenty of preinstalled software such as Python, Scratch, Sonic Pi, Java, and Mathematica.

Furthermore, more distributions, such as Ubuntu MATE, Windows 10 IoT Core, or Weather Station are meant to be installed for more specific projects such as IoT or weather stations. To conclude, the right distribution to install actually depends on your project and your expertise in Linux systems administration.

Raspberry Pi Zero W needs a MicroSD card for hosting any operating system. You will be able to write Raspbian, Noobs, Ubuntu MATE, or any other operating system you like. So, all you need to do is simply write your operating system to this MicroSD card. First of all, you have to download the image file from `https://www.raspberrypi.org/downloads/`, which usually comes as a `.zip` file. Once downloaded, unzip the zip file; the full image is about 4.5 gigabytes. Depending on your operating system, you can use different programs as follows:

- 7-Zip for Windows
- The Unarchiver for Mac
- Unzip for Linux

Now, we are ready to write the image to the MicroSD card. You can easily write the `.img` file to the MicroSD card by following one of these guides, according to your system.

For Linux users, the dd tool is recommended. Before connecting your MicroSD card with your adapter to your computer, run the following command:

```
df -h
```

Now, connect your card and run the same command again. You will see some new records. For example, if the new device is called `/dev/sdd1`, keep in your mind that the card is `/dev/sdd` (without the 1).

The next step is to use the `dd` command and copy the `.img` file to the MicroSD card. We can do this using the following command:

```
dd if=<path to your image> of=</dev/***>
```

Where `if` is the input file (image file or distribution) and `of` is the output file (MicroSD card). Again, be careful here, and only use `/dev/sdd` or whatever yours is without any numbers. If you are having trouble with this, use the full manual by referring to the link `https://www.raspberrypi.org/documentation/installation/installing-images/linux.md`. A good tool that can help you out for this job is GParted. If it is not installed on your system, you can easily install it with the following command:

```
sudo apt-get install gparted
```

Then, run `sudo gparted` to start the tool. It handles partitions very easily, and you can format, delete, or find information about all your mounted partitions.

More information about dd can be found at `https://www.raspberrypi.org/documentation/installation/installing-images/linux.md`.

- For Mac OS users, the dd tool is always recommended (`https://www.raspberrypi.org/documentation/installation/installing-images/mac.md`)
- For Windows users, the `Win32DiskImager` utility is recommended (`https://www.raspberrypi.org/documentation/installation/installing-images/windows.md`)

There are several other ways to write an image file to a microSD card. So, if you face any problems when following the preceding guides, feel free to use any other guide available on the internet. Now, assuming that everything is okay and the image is ready, you can gently plug in the MicroSD card to your Raspberry Pi Zero W board.

Remember, you can always confirm that your download was successful with the `sha1` code. In Linux systems, you can use `sha1sum` followed by the file name (the image) and print the `sha1` code. This should and must be the same as it is at the end of the official page, where you downloaded the image.

Distributors

As previously mentioned, unfortunately the Raspberry Pi Zero W board is limited to one board per user. The following is a list of the official distributors mentioned on the official Raspberry Pi website. So, depending on your location, refer to the shop accordingly.

You can either buy the Raspberry Pi Zero W board on its own or a kit containing some extra stuff. Assuming that Raspberry Pi Zero comes with a mini HDMI and needs a microSD card, you might want to buy the full kit, depending on your hardware. Also, almost everywhere, there is a kit containing the camera module. Depending again on your future projects, you might need the camera kit.

As a result, it's good advice to decide exactly what you want to do and what you plan to do with your Raspberry Pi Zero W first, and then order the board with or without extras. The following is a list of all the shops worldwide from where you can order the Raspberry Pi Zero W. In some of them, it may be out of stock, so if you plan to use a new board, since you are reading this book, buy it as soon as possible!

- UK and Ireland:
    - https://shop.pimoroni.com/collections/raspberry-pi-zero
    - https://thepihut.com/products/raspberry-pi-zero-w
    - https://www.modmypi.com/raspberry-pi/raspberry-pi-zero-board/rpi-zero-board/raspberry-pi-zero-wireless

- USA:
    - https://www.adafruit.com/pizero
    - https://www.canakit.com/raspberry-pi-zero-wireless.html
    - http://www.microcenter.com/product/475267/Zero_Wireless_Development_Board?utm_source=raspberry_pi_foundation&utm_campaign=piwinstock&utm_medium=email

- Canada:
    - https://www.canakit.com/raspberry-pi-zero-wireless.html

- Germany, Austria, and Switzerland:
    - https://buyzero.de/collections/raspberry-pi-zero-kits

- France, Spain, Italy, and Portugal:
    - https://www.kubii.fr/fr/151-pi-zero-w

- Netherlands, Belgium, and Luxembourg:
    - `https://www.kiwi-electronics.nl/raspberry-pi-zero`
- Turkey:
    - `http://www.samm.com/category/172/raspberry-pi-zero.html`
- Global:
    - `https://shop.pimoroni.com/collections/raspberry-pi-zero`
    - `https://thepihut.com/products/raspberry-pi-zero-w`
    - `https://www.adafruit.com/pizero`

Common Issues

Sometimes, working with Raspberry Pi boards can lead to issues. We have all faced some of them and hope never to face them again. The Pi Zero is so minimal that it can be tough to say whether it is working or not. Since there is no LED on the board, sometimes a quick check to see whether it is working properly or if something has gone wrong is handy.

Debugging steps

With the following steps, you will probably find its status:

1. Take your board, with nothing in any slot or socket. Remove even the microSD card!
2. Take a normal micro-USB to USB-ADATA sync cable and connect one side to your computer and the other side to the Pi's USB (not the `PWR_IN`).
3. If Zero is alive:

    - On Windows, the PC will make a ding sound to inform the presence of new hardware, and you will see `BCM2708 Boot` in **Device Manager**.
        - On Linux, with a `ID 0a5c:2763 Broadcom Corp` message from `dmesg`, try running `dmesg` in a terminal before you plug in the USB. After this, you will find a new record there.

The following is an example of the output:

```
[226314.048026] usb 4-2: new full-speed USB device number 82
using uhci_hcd [226314.213273] usb 4-2: New USB device found,
idVendor=0a5c, idProduct=2763 [226314.213280] usb 4-2: New USB
device strings: Mfr=1, Product=2, SerialNumber=0
[226314.213284] usb 4-2: Product: BCM2708 Boot
[226314.213] usb 4-2: Manufacturer: Broadcom
```

If you see any of the preceding options, so far so good, you know that Zero's not dead.

MicroSD card issue

Remember, if you boot your Raspberry and nothing is working, you may have burned your microSD card wrong. This means that your card may not contain any boot partition as it should, and it is not able to boot the first files. This problem occurs when the distribution is burned to `/dev/sdd1` and not `/dev/sdd`, as it should be. This is a common mistake, and there will be no errors on your monitor. It will just not work!

Case protection

Raspberry Pi boards are electronics, and we never place electronics on metallic surfaces or near magnetic objects. It will affect the booting operation of the Raspberry, and it will probably not work. So, a tip, spend some extra money on a Raspberry Pi case and protect your board from anything like that. There are many problems and issues when hanging your Raspberry Pi using tacks. It may be silly, but there are many who do that.

Summary

Raspberry Pi Zero W is a new, promising board allowing anyone to connect their devices to the internet and use their skills to develop projects, including software and hardware. This board is a new toy for any engineer interested in IoT, security, automation, and more! We went through an introduction to the new Raspberry Pi Zero board and the rest of its family, along with a brief analysis of some extra components that you should buy as well. In the next chapter, we will go through IoT and networking, so you can understand how to connect the Raspberry Pi Zero to your network, configure it, and start creating projects.

2
IoT and Networking

In the previous chapter, we introduced the new Raspberry Pi Zero W board. We also mentioned several accessories that someone could buy with the board to make their life easier without struggling to connect everything together. Before developing a project with that board, there is something that must be mentioned and analyzed from different perspectives. Since Raspberry Pi Zero W will be connected to the internet, it's time to talk about Internet of Things and networking. In this chapter, we will go through the following topics:

- Internet of Things
- Basic communication protocols
- Pi Zero setup
- Router setup
- Network administration
- Security

Internet of Things

Two words hiding a new world. In a few years from now, every thing and every device you own will be connected to the internet. With the new era of IoT, a huge amount of data will be collected for input on artificially intelligent algorithms or systems. Imagine if your toaster is equipped with sensors, and know what kind of bread you are using, what time you activate it, and how many times per day you want to eat toast. This information may be useless for you, but for the big companies out there willing to spend billions and risk everything on how many toasts they should produce, it is not just something, it's a game changer. So, the Internet of Things is all the things that are connected to the internet such as your computer, your lights, your fridge, your garage door, and anything else that you are able to access through the internet.

On the other side, automation is any system that thinks are make decisions. For example, a system that detects when your car arrives at your home and opens your garage door automatically is an automation. These two words will guide you through the rest of the book and will be quite helpful for the rest of your life.

Raspberry Pi, arduino and all the similar boards are made to control devices and things and connect them to the internet. So this book is about a device called Pi Zero W that allows you to handle things in your home and connect them to the internet so that you can access them from anywhere in the world:

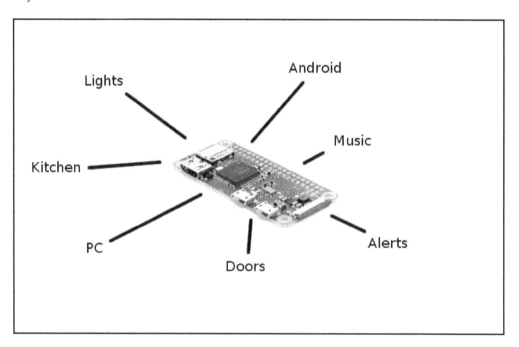

Basic communication protocols

Let's assume that we have a Raspberry Pi as our client and `https://www.facebook.com` as our server. When our client requests a web page from the server there must be some protocols, some rules that this request will be handled. With other words, there must be a specific way of transmitting and receiving data from each other. **Internet Protocols** (**IP**) are exactly the rules according to which a client and a server talk.

There are some basic IP with which the current browsers communicate with servers and get data. However, when we talk about IoT and low power hardware, we cannot keep these protocols and use them. As a result, it is important to go through some basic stuff and know the idea behind all the communications out there.

Internet protocols

Since this section is not what the book is about, we will go through some basic protocols that we all have used (maybe without knowing). HTTP protocol is used when requesting a web page. For example, when someone types `https://facebook.com/`, he requests a web page called *facebook*. FTP protocol is used when a client connects in a file server. For example, when someone types `ftp.ntua.gr/`, he connects in a server where there are just files and no website or blog. In addition, TCP and UDP are protocols used for transmitting data. UDP is used for video call or voice call, where we need a huge amount of data transmitted, whereas, TCP is used for HTTP request or similar actions.

The reason we went through these protocols is because if you read further about them you will see that every single one of them has quite many bytes necessary to work properly, which means power over the cable, which in turn means energy consumption. So, people have thought that in Internet of Things we do not need the existing protocols and there are some new protocols specifically for IoT.

IoT Protocols

IoT has created a new need of advance protocols in many layers. There is not the need to device communication protocols, semantic, identification, infrastructure, and more. There are plenty of protocols developed for this kind of work and no one's quite sure about what will and will not work perfectly at the future. IoT is one of the top research interested in many universities and very complicated. At this section of the chapter, we will go through the following basic IoT protocols necessary for working on related projects.

- Bluetooth
- Zigbee
- Z-Wave
- 6LowPan
- Thread
- Wi-Fi

- Celludar
- NFC
- LoRaWAN

Bluetooth

This communication protocol is short range and is known to almost anyone. It is very important and expected to be the key for wearable products. Raspberry Pi Zero W support bluetooth and this is a great opportunity for you to create projects and be familiar with this protocol. The new protocol **Bluetooth Low Energy** (**BLE**) or **Bluetooth Smart** is a significant protocol for Internet of Things and even if it has similar range it was firstly designed offering reduced power consumption. To conclude with, when talking about IoT, it is all about energy consumption. Your Raspberry Pi Zero W may work forever if it is plugged in the home power source, but if you are using it for wearables such as a smart watch, then the power consumption matters a lot.

Bluetooth is working at the frequency of 2.4 GHz (ISM) with a range of 20-150m (BLE) and with data rates up to 1Mbps (Smart/BLE).

Zigbee

The **Zigbee** protocol is also works at 2.4 GHz and is based on the IEEE 802.15.4 protocol. It exchanges at low data rates over a restricted range of 100 m range. As a result, Zigbee is suitable for homes or small businesses. In addition, this protocol has some advantages offering low power operation and high security with scalability. Zigbee data rates reach up to 250 Kbps.

Z-Wave

Z-Wave is a low power RF communications technology designed for smart homes and automation. Data rates are up to 100 kbit/s and it operates in the sub-1 GHz band. It supports full mesh networks without the need for a central node that coordinates the data flow. The frequency is at 900 MHz (ISM) with a range of up to 30 m. Overall, it is a good protocol for device communication in home automation.

6LowPAN

6LowPAN is a network protocol designed encapsulation and header compression mechanisms. It is frequently used among other protocols such as Ethernet or Wi-Fi, and the advantage of this protocol, is that it supports IPv6, which is the goal of almost everyone. Designed for home automation, it promises to produce complex control systems and to communicate with devices via a low power wireless network.

NFC

Near field communication (**NFC**) is a technology that enables a close transfer or interaction between two devices. Almost all of the latest Android and IoS devices support this technology and it is quite useful for identification or trigger situations. It will be used for home automation or for check in security businesses. It actually extends the capability of card technology and enables devices to share information. It works in frequency or 13.56 MHz (ISM) and has a range or 10 cm.

Wi-Fi

Wi-Fi is almost everywhere. We have all connected to a network via Wi-Fi so we understand pretty much how it is working. It handles quite high quantities of data and currently the common Wi-Fi standard is 802.11n, which offers throughput of hundreds of megbits/sec. However, since every good thing has a disadvantage, Wi-Fi is very energy consuming so this protocol is not very good for IoT when talking about wearables or anything else in which every consumption is crucial. It works 2.4 GHz or 5GHz and supports up to 50 m.

LoRaWAN

LoRaWAN targets **Wide Area Network** (**WAN**) applications and it is a low cost protocol with scalability. Ideal for smart cities, it can connect many devices together with data rates from 0.3 to 50 Kbps. Its range is from 5 km to 15 km if there is no obstacle.

Connecting your Pi

At this point, we have to connect the Raspberry Pi Zero W to the internet. To do this, we first have to understand how internet works. How everything's connected and how we will manage to plug in our Raspberry Pi. This section of the book will demonstrate how to guide for a variety of routers. Since every process is different, I will try to describe the basic idea here and hopefully you will be able to find your solution.

Pi Zero W setup

Firstly, in order to follow the rest of the book, you have to connect your Raspberry Pi zero to a monitor using HDMI and then do the following. Create a new folder with the name ssh at /boot folder and restart your pi. You will be prompted with a message about SSH. If this is done, then you can continue the rest of the chapter and work remotely using SSH as described next.

Also notice that you need the latest image. Older images from your old Raspberry Pi board or anything else will not work and there will be no Wi-Fi adaptor found. So have in mind that you need to install the latest image.

The internet

The internet consists of edges and nodes. Every computer out there is a node and every cable is an edge. Wireless communications have an *invisible* cable, which is called air:

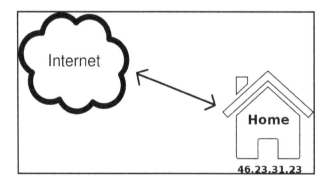

As you can see in the preceding diagram, we can visualize internet as a cloud. We don' t really have to understand what's in there. Your **Internet Service Provider** (**ISP**) provides you with your internet connection. Thus, you usually have a router in your home. Since there are billions of nodes connected to the internet communicating over protocols and sending/receiving hundreds of messages, there must be a way of identifying who is who. This means that the router must have a unique identification, like the address in your house. This address is called the IP address or Internet protocol and there are two protocols. The old and classic one is version4 and the new one is version6. No further explanation is needed for this, just remember that every home has a router and every router has a unique IPv4 address. So now everyone from outside your house knows that every packet in your IPv4 address will reach your router.

Local network

Let's assume that a packet has arrived at your router. It's crucial to understand what exactly is going on and how the router decides the destination of the packet. In your local network (your home), there may be 10 devices such as tablets, smartphones, PC, and laptops. The router has to decide in which of them it should send the packet. This is done with the **Network Address Translation** (**NAT**) protocol. So somehow it chooses one device and it sends the packet. Every single device in your home has an IP address. It is not the same as your home IP address that we mentioned earlier. When you connect a device in your local network (router), it automatically gets an IP address such as `192.168.1.101`.

To sum up, the internet consists of clients (homes) and servers (endpoints). For example, a client is your home and a server is `https://www.facebook.com`. A client is connected to the server through some nodes (switches) usually with cables and there are plenty of them out there. What we described earlier is the internet. Going further, the local network consists of a switch, which in this case is called router and some devices such as your smartphone or laptop. Your router is responsible for delivering anything that comes to your home to the appropriate device. Your router and every single device has an IP address.

The structure of your local network is a tree. This means that everything starts from the router and expands. You may have another local network in your garage or in your yard. For example, you can see in the following screenshot that my network consists of some devices and another switch which consists of some more devices.

In the following screenshot, we can see a page of my router and it must be crystal clear that apart from the Wi-Fi there are two Ethernet ports enabled of which one is connected to a computer and the other to something called a switch that has two devices. The first one is again a computer and the second is our Raspberry Pi Zero W. You can find the IP of the Raspberry Pi in the following screenshot:

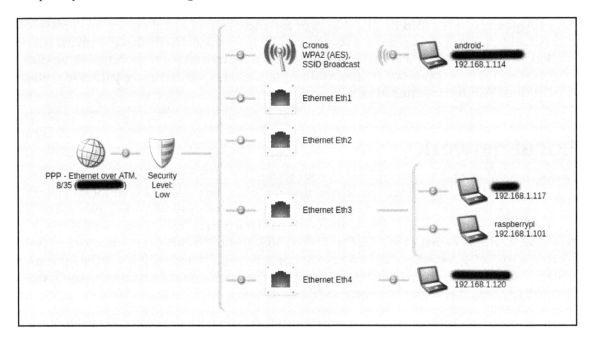

Your Raspberry Pi Zero W will be one device connected to your router and will have an IP address like every other device. This device depends on your router. Usually, the IP addresses in your home will be of the format 192.168.1.X, where X is in the range of 1 to 254, but even if the numbers differ, the idea is the same. Usually, since the router is the first device connected to the internet, it has an IP address 192.168.1.1, the second device may have 192.168.1.2, the third device 192.168.1.3, and so on as you can see in the upcoming image my raspberry, which has the IP 192.168.1.101. All of the preceding information is important because we will connect to our Raspberry Pi using SSH over the network. But of course to connect to it we will have to find it first.

Port forwarding

At this point, the difference of a local network and the whole internet should be crystal clear. Now we will see how to connect to our pi from the outside world? If we connect to our home IP address, we will get nothing because our router is not a server, it is just a router. Our server is the Raspberry Pi, which is located inside our home with a local IP address. The answer to this question is port forwarding. Unfortunately, not all routers support this but this is necessary for connecting to your Raspberry Pi from the outside world. If you have a router that does not support port forwarding, consider buying a good one since good routers are equipped with options for better security and connection handling. Next, you can see a screenshot, where we have made a route from the outside world to a specific IP address in the local network. To create a new route, you have to login to your router interface and click on the tab named **Port forwarding**. To find more about how you can do this, download and read your router manual:

Description	Traffic Coming from	External Port	Internal Port	Local Host
Rasp Server	Any Host PPP - Ethernet over ATM, 8/35	TCP 1770 ⇨	2880	raspberrypi (192.168.1.101) ▼

From the preceding screenshot, we can understand that any connection from all over the world coming to your home at port 1770 will be redirected to port 2880 at the computer with IP 192.168.1.101, which is our Raspberry Pi Zero.

What's left is a server that will respond and will be running in our Raspberry Pi Zero W.

Connecting to the internet

Assuming that we made port forwarding all out outdoor connection to our Raspberry Pi Zero W, we can easily connect to it from anywhere in the world by simply using the external IP of our home. For example, if you google find my ip and come up with a result like 45.12.64.23, then all you need to do is close the Wi-Fi connection from your mobile phone and using the data try to go to http://45.12.64.23/ (obviously change that to your IP address). You should be able to communicate with your Raspberry Pi like that at port 80. HTTP port is the number 80 and this is the port that you are requesting when you type in a URL such as http://XXX. You can specify your port in the URL by typing http://45.12.64.23:<port> and as a result you are connecting your device with your home in port <port>, where port is a number from 1000 to 4000. Actually, there are more ports but if you are not an advance user, stay at this range.

Networking administration

In this section, we will go through some basic Linux commands that will help determine future problems. Feel free to come back here and read this again. There are many commands that we can execute in a terminal to debug our project or the Raspberry Pi Zero W communication setup that we have made.

At first, the most basic command is `ifconfig`. The `ifconfig` command outputs some interfaces and plenty of information about them. For example, you can easily find what is the IP of your Raspberry Pi Zero W device is by simply typing:

```
Ifconfig
```

As shown in the following screenshot, the IP address can easily be found. If you see no IP address, it means that your Raspberry Pi Zero W device is connected to the internet:

```
pi@raspberrypi:~ $ ifconfig
eth0      Link encap:Ethernet  HWaddr b8:27:eb:ed:23:bb
          inet addr:192.168.1.101  Bcast:192.168.1.255  Mask:255.255.255.0
          inet6 addr: fe80::fed5:3971:f6a8:61a6/64 Scope:Link
          UP BROADCAST RUNNING MULTICAST  MTU:1500  Metric:1
          RX packets:483259 errors:0 dropped:40 overruns:0 frame:0
          TX packets:158544 errors:0 dropped:0 overruns:0 carrier:0
          collisions:0 txqueuelen:1000
          RX bytes:135705578 (129.4 MiB)  TX bytes:19824896 (18.9 MiB)

lo        Link encap:Local Loopback
          inet addr:127.0.0.1  Mask:255.0.0.0
          inet6 addr: ::1/128 Scope:Host
          UP LOOPBACK RUNNING  MTU:65536  Metric:1
          RX packets:625 errors:0 dropped:0 overruns:0 frame:0
          TX packets:625 errors:0 dropped:0 overruns:0 carrier:0
          collisions:0 txqueuelen:1
          RX bytes:56274 (54.9 KiB)  TX bytes:56274 (54.9 KiB)

wlan0     Link encap:Ethernet  HWaddr b8:27:eb:b8:76:ee
          inet6 addr: fe80::bc24:b350:3b5b:c186/64 Scope:Link
          UP BROADCAST MULTICAST  MTU:1500  Metric:1
          RX packets:102707 errors:0 dropped:102707 overruns:0 frame:0
          TX packets:0 errors:0 dropped:0 overruns:0 carrier:0
          collisions:0 txqueuelen:1000
          RX bytes:36998689 (35.2 MiB)  TX bytes:0 (0.0 B)
```

The next command that helps when we have networking issues is `ping`. With `ping`, we can determine whether a server is down or up. In other words, by pinging at a server which is up we can determine whether you are connected to the internet or not. In the following example, we will ping `www.google.com` and see whether we get a response or not. Type the following command:

```
ping -c 3 www.google.com
```

If everything is okay, you should have a result similar to the following, where we can see that there are two responses with 64 bytes each:

```
pi@raspberrypi:~ $ ping -c 3 www.google.com
PING www.google.com (216.58.208.36) 56(84) bytes of data.
64 bytes from fra15s12-in-f36.1e100.net (216.58.208.36): icmp_seq=1 ttl=54 time=135 ms
64 bytes from fra15s12-in-f36.1e100.net (216.58.208.36): icmp_seq=3 ttl=54 time=164 ms

--- www.google.com ping statistics ---
3 packets transmitted, 2 received, 33% packet loss, time 2005ms
rtt min/avg/max/mdev = 135.914/150.445/164.977/14.536 ms
pi@raspberrypi:~ $ _
```

The `-c 3` argument that we gave means that we request only three pings and then stop the command.

Now we will start a simple server in our Raspberry Pi so we can verify that everything is OK and we have access to our Pi from all over the world. To do that, we use the Python language and we will start a daemon that Python allows us. If you do not have Python installed, type the following command:

```
sudo apt-get install python
```

Then type the following:

```
python
```

Verify that everything is OK. The next step is to start the server. To do that, we need to type the following:

```
python -m SimpleHTTPServer 8000
```

If everything went well, we will have a result similar to the following, where we can see that the server is up and running at port `8000`:

```
▓▓▓▓▓▓▓▓ ~ $ python -m SimpleHTTPServer 8000
Serving HTTP on 0.0.0.0 port 8000 ...
_
```

Connect for command execution

In this section, we will see how we can connect to your Raspberry Pi Zero W over the network using SSH. SSH stands for secure shell and is an easy way of connecting to almost any device like our Raspberry Pi Zero W. Firstly, we have to define the IP address of our raspberry as shown earlier. Assuming that the IP address is `192.168.1.101`, all that we have to do is use an `ssh` client.

In Linux and Mac operating systems, just open a terminal and type the following:

```
ssh <user>@<ip-address>
```

Here, `<user>` is `pi` and `<ip-address>` is `192.168.1.101`:

```
                              pi@raspberrypi: ~                         –   ⌀   ⊗
pi@raspberrypi:~ $ ssh pi@192.168.1.101
The authenticity of host '192.168.1.101 (192.168.1.101)' can't be established.
ECDSA key fingerprint is da:18:6e:36:10:fb:5e:e1:65:09:ef:82:0e:2d:42:14.
Are you sure you want to continue connecting (yes/no)? yes_
```

After that, just type your password and hit *Enter*:

```
                              pi@raspberrypi: ~                         –   ⌀   ⊗
pi@raspberrypi:~ $ ls
BBChat    Documents  Music     Public     Videos
Desktop   Downloads  Pictures  Templates  sketchbook
pi@raspberrypi:~ $ _
```

You can now see that the `bash` has changed and we are in our Raspberry Pi Zero W.

Automatic authentication

Sometimes it is useful to automatically authenticate ourselves over the Raspberry Pi board. This means that we will not be prompted to enter our password or anything else. The next script that is named `cpi` (connecting to Raspberry Pi) is a useful command to easily get access to our board over SSH. Actually, the script consists of just a single line. Create a new file named `cpi` and type the following command:

```
ssh pi@<Raspberry Pi Address>
```

Save it to the `/bin` folder with `sudo`. Next, you need to create an `rsa` keygen and transfer the public key (`name.pub`) to the `.ssh/authorized_keys` file in Raspberry Pi Zero W.

In Windows operating systems, the easiest way of doing this is to use an `ssh` client such as PuTTY . You can download PuTTY for free using the following link:

`http://www.chiark.greenend.org.uk/~sgtatham/putty/latest.html`

Notice that there is no need for installation. Just open the executable that you have just downloaded and setup your connection. You need to specify the **Host Name** or **IP address** of your Raspberry Pi device and set **Port** 22 for all SSH connections (the default port). Click on **Open** and then you will be prompted to enter your username, which is pi, and your password, which is raspberry. After hitting *Enter*, you should easily log in to your Raspberry Pi device:

Connecting for file transfer

Sometimes, we are against the problem of transferring data and files at and from our Raspberry Pi. SSH cannot be used for that, so the following section will describe ways that you can easily transfer files from and to your raspberry pi.

FileZilla

FileZilla software can be downloaded on either Windows or Linux and it is pretty simple. For Windows you can download it from https://filezilla-project.org/download.php and for Linux you can use the same link or type the following command:

```
sudo apt-get install filezilla
```

After installing this software, all you have to do is type the IP address of the Raspberry Pi, the port (which be default is 22), and the username/password which usually are pi/raspberry.

Click on connect and you should see two sections. The left section are the local files in your computer and the right section are the remote files (Raspberry Pi Zero). Simply, use drag and drop files from one section to another.

After connecting to the Raspberry Pi Board, you should see something like this:

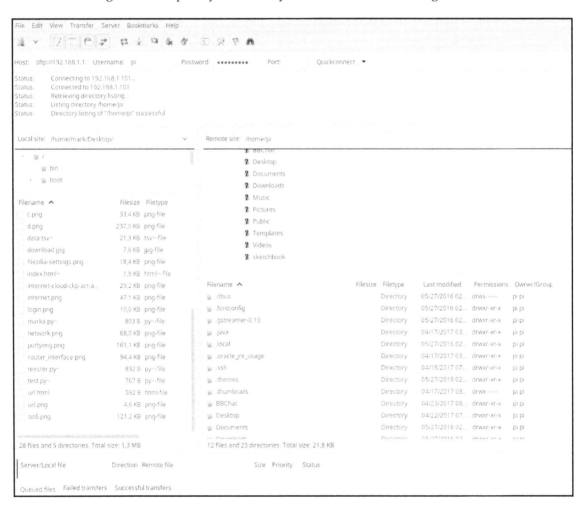

SCP

In Linux operating systems, there is one command called `scp` and it can transfer files from and to a remote server. This is useful because sometimes we do not have a graphical user interface and `scp` is our only option. USB drives work as well but we suppose that we transfer files over the network. `scp` is a command-line tool and is easy to work with.

To transfer a file from your computer to a remote server (Raspberry Pi) type the following command:

```
scp <file-transferred> <user>@<pi-address>:<where to put>
```

```
          ~/Desktop $ scp url.png pi@192.168.1.102:/home/pi/
pi@192.168.1.102's password:
url.png                                   100% 4528      4.4KB/s   00:00
```

Here `<user>` is `pi` and `<pi-address>` is the IP address of Raspberry Pi. Notice that there are `:` between the IP address and the file transferred. If you are inside a folder and want to copy all the files, replace `<file-transfer>` with `*`.

On the other hand, to transfer from your remote server (Raspberry Pi) to your local machine type the following:

```
scp username@remote:/file/to/send /where/to/put
scp <user>@<pi-address>:<file-transferred> <where to put>
```

You can always view more about a Linux command using the following command:

```
man <linux-command>
```

Secure the Raspberry Pi and remove others

In the last section of this chapter, we will talk about security. Raspberry Pi Zero W is great but no one wants to just plug it in your router and let others control your lights, your coffee machine, and anything else you have connected there. To begin with, the truth is that you cannot be secure from anyone. This means that there are levels of security that you should consider. At this point, you should consider from whom you want to be secured. For example, there are techniques for securing your Raspberry from your family, from your friends, from anyone in your house, from typical users on the internet, from advance users on the internet, and from NSA.

Firewall

Almost every router has a firewall option. Firewall is a system that is able to filter all incoming connections and choose whether every single one of them is OK to let it pass to your network or not. In the following screenshot, you can see the **Firewall** option at my router settings. It may differ from your router, but it usually exists under the **Security** tab in the menu:

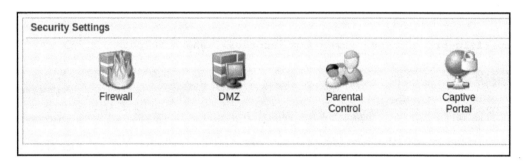

Furthermore, if we click on Firewall, there is an option to activate it or deactivate it. There is also the option of how strong our firewall will be. LOW firewall means that it will almost let everything pass through your network. **HIGH** firewall means that it will almost alert and prevent incoming connecting from going through your network. In case you think that **HIGH** is always the best option, it is not. Sometimes when you play online games or use applications over the network, you have to disable your firewall. So keep in mind that sometimes depending on your network you need to disable your firewall and this means that yes you are more vulnerable that before. So never show your IP or do nasty things:

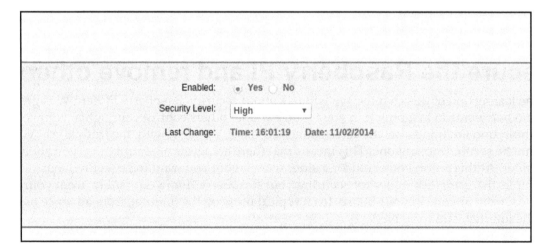

There is another firewall on your operating system. Windows has a default firewall that you many need to disable too when creating software related to your machine. To conclude with, never disable anything if all is working fine. I am just mentioning them in case of any issues with networking and connection failures.

Last but not least, when making your Raspberry Pi Zero internet connected, start using passwords with at least eight characters, including a special character, number, and a capital.

Summary

In this chapter, we went through some basics of networking, and saw how you can connect your Raspberry Pi over the network. We also talked about getting access over the internet, and about IoT protocols.

In the next chapter, we will start building our first project with the new Raspberry Pi Zero W board and look at more practical things using all the knowledge from the previous chapters.

3
Chatbot

Nowadays, chatbots are very popular and used by huge companies to researchers to anyone who has a passion to learn and use automated responses. A chatbot is a system that has the ability to respond to your questions in an automated way. There are smart chatbots and dump ones. The difference between them is that a smart chatbot is well trained and has the ability to understand the language and syntax that you type and responds accordingly, whereas the dump one responds in an almost specific way according to a question. In this chapter, we will create a simple and easy chatbot using Raspberry Pi Zero W. We will go through the following topics in this chapter:

- User input
- Server installation
- and networking services
- Security

User input

In this section, we will see some basic ways in which a user can message or talk to a bot. There are several ways that anyone can talk to their bot depending on the operating system that they are using. Raspberry Pi Zero W can be used as the bot or as the user input device. Raspberry Pi 3 was a good board for creating even a Facebook bot, but this new Raspberry Pi Zero W board is not recommended to be used for difficult purposes such as running a huge bot. So, what we will do in this project is a simple demonstration of how things work and how we can develop a bot from scratch.

In this section, we will develop a web page to use as the user input device. With this, you can easily develop an Android application or a speech recognition system. Everything will work fine as long as the program has a string of what the user said as output. The web page will be developed in HTML and a bit of CSS.

Server installation

Before creating a website, we have to decide where we will develop the site and with what tools. I recommend using your desktop or laptop and not Raspberry Pi as the main computer to work on. Also, try using a text editor, such as Sublime Text, since they will help you a lot. This is my preferred style; feel free to choose yours.

To develop a website, we need a server, and we can easily use a XAMPP or LAMPP server on a Windows, Linux, or Mac system. Download the package from `https://www.apachefriends.org/download.html`.

After this, install the package on your system, and start the control panel. In Linux systems, you can start the services by opening a Terminal and typing the following command:

```
sudo /opt/lampp/lampp start
```

As we can see in the following screenshot, Apache, MySQL, and ProFTPD have started, since they responded with `already running` messages:

```
mark@zeus ~ $ sudo /opt/lampp/lampp start
[sudo] password for mark:
Starting XAMPP for Linux 7.0.15-0...
XAMPP: Starting Apache...already running.
XAMPP: Starting MySQL...already running.
XAMPP: Starting ProFTPD...already running.
mark@zeus ~ $ _
```

Use this code if you want to close the services type:

```
sudo /opt/lampp/lampp stop
```

The following screenshot is what you will see as a result:

```
mark@zeus ~ $ sudo /opt/lampp/lampp stop
Stopping XAMPP for Linux 7.0.15-0...
XAMPP: Stopping Apache...ok.
XAMPP: Stopping MySQL...ok.
XAMPP: Stopping ProFTPD...ok.
mark@zeus ~ $ _
```

In case you want to restart, type the following command:

```
sudo /opt/lampp/lampp restart
```

In the following screenshot, we can see that the services were not running, but they had started. If they were running instead of not running, we would have received the ok message:

```
mark@zeus ~ $ sudo /opt/lampp/lampp restart
Restarting XAMPP for Linux 7.0.15-0...
XAMPP: Stopping Apache...not running.
XAMPP: Stopping MySQL...not running.
XAMPP: Stopping ProFTPD...not running.
XAMPP: Starting Apache...ok.
XAMPP: Starting MySQL...ok.
XAMPP: Starting ProFTPD...ok.
mark@zeus ~ $ _
```

Note that XAMPP will be using port 80, so it is recommended that you close Skype or any other program running on these ports. After starting the XAMPP services, you can open Skype or any other program again with no problem. The common problem is that they conflict with the ports that are using same port as Skype or when we stream with any similar program open and use the port needed for XAMPP.

If everything goes OK, the only thing that you have to do is open a browser, such as Firefox, and enter http://localhost/dashboard/.

You will see a website like the following, which is the dashboard of the XAMPP server:

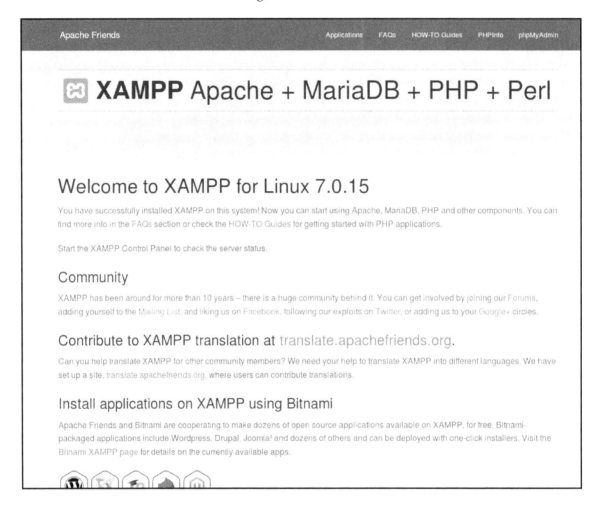

At this point, we are clear that the Apache server is what we need for writing a website using HTML, CSS, and PHP code. MySQL service, on the other hand, is what we need to create a database.

The folder in which we will save our website is `/opt/lampp/htdocs`. Proceed to this folder using the following command:

```
cd /opt/lampp/htdocs/
```

Create a new directory with the name chatUI:

```
sudo mkdir chatUI
```

Now, run ls, and you should have a directory in the htdocs folder. Confirm this by navigating to your browser and typing http://localhost/chatUI/. You should see something similar to the following screenshot:

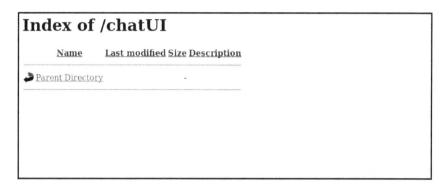

Now, you can see that nothing is listed in the directory as we have no files in our project. Create a file named index.php with your favorite editor and use the following code:

```
<html>
<head></head>
<body>
This is my website
</body>
</html>
```

The result that you should see after reloading the website is as follows:

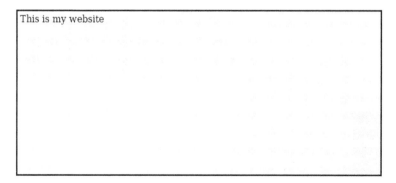

Now, since this chapter is not about web development, I have written some code so that a user can place a question and receive an answer from the server.

The chatbot development

A chatbot is a bot that has an interaction with something; for example, a user can submit a query and the bot will respond according to the query:

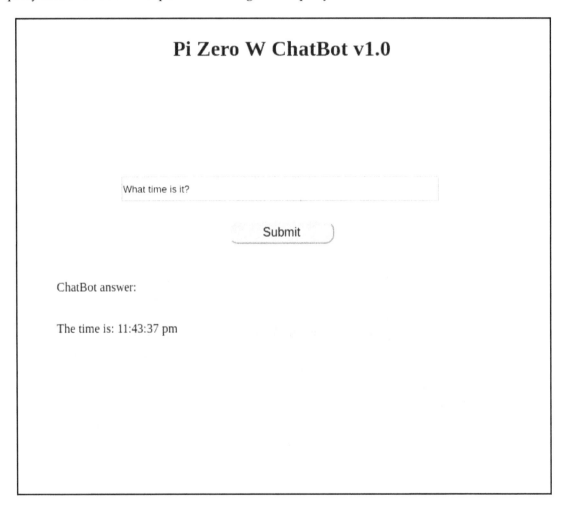

Next, you will find a code that demonstrates this scenario. It is a website of our chatbot using HTML, CSS, and PHP language. Let's go through the code line by line.

The following lines create a page title and link the file with the CSS stylesheet file. The title can be found on the browser tab of the chatbot website. Also, `style.css` must be located in the same folder as the `index.php` file. If not, you have to add the full path of the `style.css` file, as follows:

```
<title>PI Zero W – Chatbot</title>
<link rel="stylesheet" href="style.css" />
```

Next, we have to write some PHP code. First, we do a check to see whether `usertext` is set. This means that if the user has typed something and clicked on the button, then the `usertext` field is set. We get the data using the `$_POST` method, and then, we check whether the user input is one of the known questions:

```php
<?php
    if( isset($_POST['usertext'])) {
      $input = $_POST['usertext'];
      switch($input) {
        case "hello":
          $outdata = "Hello there! What can I do for you?";
          break;
        case "hi":
            $outdata = "Hey! What' up?";
            break;
        case "how are you?":
          $outdata = "I am fine! You?";
          break;
        case "what time is it?":
            $timezone = date_default_timezone_get();
            date_default_timezone_set($timezone);
            $date = date('h:i:s a', time());
            $outdata = "The time is: " . $date;
            break;
        case "who are you?":
            $outdata = "I am your lovely chatbot!";
            break;    default:
        $outdata = "Oup's  I didn' t get that!";
          break;
      }
    }
  ?>
```

Note that with this code, we have not built a smart chatbot or an artificially intelligent bot. To do that, we have to write many more lines of code. In this section, we will see how to create a simple chatbot so that you will be familiar with the idea.

In case we want an advanced chatbot, we have to use a database here. Instead of using the switch statement, we should create a query to our database and ask the question that the user submitted. You can read more about databases in the next section of this chapter.

Our body part consists of two sections or divisions: the header `div` and the main `div`. The header `div` is the main title of our web page and the main `div` is an HTML form that allows the user to submit a question to the chatbot. Inside the main div, we have an answer div that is actually the invisible box, where the bot answer will be displayed. We print nothing if the question is not set, and we print the bot answer if the page is reloaded and the question is set:

```
<body>
  <div id="header">
    Pi Zero W ChatBot v1.0
  </div>
  <div id="main">
    <form method="POST" action="">
      <input id="userinput" type="text" name="usertext" value="Type
here...">
      <br><br>
      <input id="submitbutton" type="submit" value="Submit">
    </form>
    <div id="answer">
      ChatBot answer:<br><br><br>
      <?php
        if(!isset($outdata)) {
          echo "";
        }else {
          echo $outdata;
        }
      ?>
    </div>
  </div>
</body>
```

As you have already seen, we created a website and uploaded the files into the Raspberry Pi board `www` or `htdocs` folder. Our website is available for all local networks. This means that if you want to access it from anywhere else you will not be able to do that. You have to create a rule in your router settings and port forward an external port to your internal port. The external port can be whatever you want, for example, 2823, but the internal port of your Raspberry Pi must be port `80`.

Chat services

There are several available chatbot services all over the internet. You can easily create a chatbot by registering yourself on one of the following services or by downloading any necessary libraries. Let's go through some very interesting chatbots that you should have in mind; and make sure you keep them at the back of your mind for future projects.

Chatfuel

Chatfuel is good if you have a page on Facebook. It is actually a bot for Facebook Messenger and Telegram. The installation steps are very easy and guide you step by step in making your own chatbot, without any coding needed. You can edit a response for any question asked, and the best part of it is that it is free if you stay under 1,00,000 messages per month. In the following screenshot, we can see the interface of the Chatfuel service:

Source: `https://bbvaopen4u.com/`

Frow XO

Flow XO, on the other hand, offers a wider array of features and integrations. You have a visual bot builder with a graphical user interface, such as Chatfuel (mentioned previously), for a standard plan of $19/month for 15 bots or active flows and 2,500 interactions. It supports many additional features, such as multitalk, for more than one user. In the following screenshot, we can see the interface, where the user is prompted to choose a service:

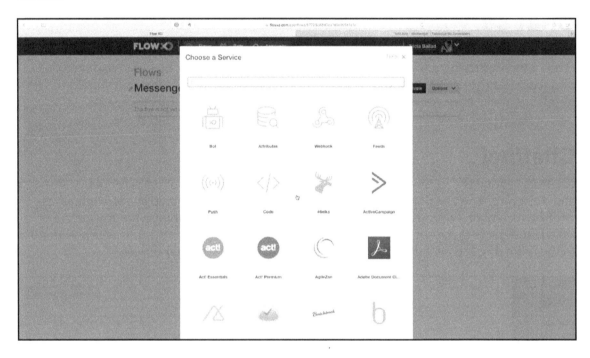

Source: https://i.ytimg.com

Converse

Converse is a new service available for everyone. It is up and coming, with amazing features. It is a future-promising service with which you will be able to talk and pay. This platform is free for anyone, and it has more features than Facebook Messenger.

Facebook messenger

Another option is to control your Raspberry Pi board using Facebook Messenger. Facebook allows you to connect your messenger chat platform with Raspberry and just type commands or anything you want and execute them on the Raspberry Pi board. In this section, we will mention the whole idea of the preceding scenario as an alternative option. The user communicates through the Facebook page made for the Raspberry Pi using the Facebook API with the actual Raspberry Pi board, which should be connected to the internet. As a result, we have two requirements for this project:

- A Raspberry Pi board connected to the internet
- A Dataplicity remote terminal with wormhole enabled

At first, you have to create a Facebook account and a Facebook page. Then, go to `https://developers.facebook.com/`, log in using the administrator account, and create an app. Then, you have to download the appropriate code to the Raspberry Pi board and connect it to the WebHook.

Since this project is not the main goal of the chapter, if you are interested in it, you can follow the instructions at `https://www.hackster.io/dataplicity/use-facebook-to-control-your-raspberry-pi-terminal-2be038`.

Google cleverbot

Google, in 2012, developed a library that provides a binding for Cleverbot. It supports opening a chat session, asking stuff, and receiving answers, simple as that. In 2012, there were not so many libraries out there, so this is a great opportunity to go through the old stuff that developers were working on. You can find more information at `https://code.google.com/archive/p/pycleverbot/`, as shown in the following screenshot:

An example of the usage is shown here:

```
import cleverbot
mycb=cleverbot.Session()
mycb.Ask("Hello there") 'Hello.'
mycb.Ask('Whats going on?')
'Not much. What is your name?' ```
```

Unfortunately, as you can easily see, work on this project stopped in 2012. No one knows what will happen or whether Google is preparing something else, but this is Google, and almost all Google software is great. It is worth taking a look at this library.

Secure data transfer

When building a chatbot yourself and not using one of the hundred services available, you have to keep the subject of security in mind. Firstly, when building software like this, depending on the sensitivity of your software and depending on what information someone can extract from the bot, you might need to add some more security layers, such as user authentication. You can easily create or find online, some code with a login page before accessing the user input web page. Secondly, it is recommended that you create more security checks in your code. If you just have an if statement that checks whether the user said *password*, then the user might submit some code and perform an SQL injection. An SQL injection is performed in websites that operate with a database. The attacker can easily submit an SQL statement and modify or get access to the database tables, even if he shouldn't be able to. Security measures such as the preceding ones are crucial to ensure that you and only you will access your bot.

Over the network, you can use the *Wireshark* software to capture packets and watch the content of each packet. There is more software available that is similar to Wireshark, and all of it belongs to a category of security software named network sniffers. Anyone in your network can sniff your network and capture packets that you are sending to your Raspberry Pi board. As a result, it is always recommended that you use HTTPS and not the simple HTTP protocol for your services, especially if you develop a chatbot and make it available on the internet for everyone.

Summary

In this chapter, you learned about chatbots, how they work, and how they interact with the user. You also saw some new chatbot services available for everyone that you can use and build great projects with. In the next chapter, we will change our topic and enter into the world of robotics. By the end of the next chapter, you will be able to develop your own mobile robot and use Facebook Messenger or any other service to control it.

4
Mobile Robot

In this chapter, we will create and learn how to control, via an Android application, a simple mobile robot. The mobile robot will be able to move in all directions and give feedback to the Android device or the computer with which it will be connected. Almost all the robots follow the same principal. As a result, if you understand how a robot works, you can easily adjust your robot to anything you want: Create another one, develop the old one, and build an entire world with robots. In this chapter, we will cover all the necessary fundamentals for building your first wireless robot with Raspberry Pi Zero W. To conclude, we will go through the following topics:

- Fundamentals of robotics
- Hardware overview
- Programming the controller
- Future ideas

Fundamentals of robotics

A mobile robot belongs to the wheeled robots category and is usually equipped with wheels or crawlers. For the sake of simplicity, in this chapter, we will develop a two-wheeled mobile robot. In fact, our robot will have three wheels but the third one will be neutral and will be used for the overall robot balance. So, the actual actuators are the two front motors and thus we call it a two-wheeled robot.

Any robot mechanism consists of actuators and links. An actuator is a motor or anything the produces thrust and torque. A link, on the other hand, is the hardware part that links the actuator with the chassis. The basic principle is very simple and inside every robot there are motors and links. In this project, we will build a two-wheel mobile robot, which consists of two actuators. In other words, our actuators are simple DC motors, which produce the necessary torque to turn the wheel and move the robot. Every simple actuator is linked with screws or double tape with the chassis described next. Our third wheel is neutral and follows the total horizontal thrust and vertical turn of the actuators.

When building a DIY robot, it is important to define the reason. If you want to just build a robot and play around, which is great and full of fun, you do not have to care about bugs and errors. However, if you want to build a robot for research purposes, for example, for your university, then you need to pick and choose your hardware with care. We will talk about it later on, but it is important to have in mind the total budget and the final purpose. For the sake of simplicity in this project, we will go through a simple and cheap mobile robot, which will produce errors as you will see later. Professional robotics components are expensive but minimize the total system error.

Furthermore, if you want to build a robot for research purposes, then keep in mind that you may need to buy hardware with as many specifications as you can have. Buying a motor that you have no idea about the voltage, RPM, inner resistance and all the other specifications will only make your work harder. There is always the option of *test and find what you want* but why bother when you can pick another motor with all the information you want. With that told, an example of two motors will clear any concerns that you might have. The right DC motor is cheap and costs $ 2.50, while the left DC motor is a little more expensive and costs $ 14. There is no big difference in price but under the description of the left motor we can find the Inner resistance, max Amps, and more information that will be useful in our project:

DC motors

A DC motor mostly consists of coils and gears. But to understand what really is a DC motor and how it works, we need to look inside of it and understand the physics behind it. Two magnets with opposite polarity are attracted to each other but with the same polarity they oppose each other. There are various DC motors on the market, but to understand the idea behind magical torque produced we will go through a simple DC motor, like the motor we will use later on. The following image shows a simple DC motor, taken apart:

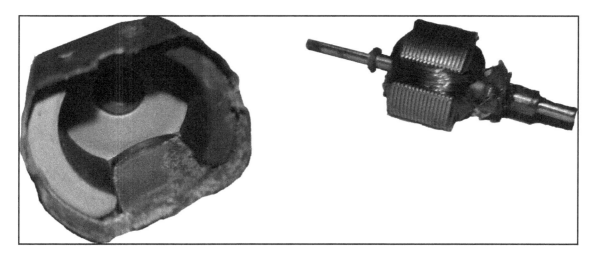

On the left-side of the image, we can see the outer part of the motor where there are two magnets with different polarity. On the right-side of the image, we can see the shaft, wrapped with coil. Applying voltage to the coil, makes it act like a small magnet. This coil-created magnet opposes or attracts the fixed magnet on the outer part. As a result, we have the final rotation of the shaft. We usually add some kind of gears or similar components to the shaft and control the exact rounds per minute (RPM) that we want.

The more current the coil has as input, the stronger the coil-magnet is. The stronger the coil-magnet is, the more RPM the shaft has.

Torque

When talking for DC motors and mobile robots, usually we need to control the robot with low RPM. In other words, we do not need a shaft that spins with 10.000 RPM. Notice that the actual motor may spin with 10.000, but we need a way to reduce that RPM at the final wheel mount point. So, when we place the wheels or any other similar component to the motor, we will have a normal and controlled speed. This is different in the brushless motors that quadcopters use. In quadcopters and other flying machines, we do not need torque, but we need speed. One easy way to reduce the actual RPM of a motor is using gears. The following image shows the inside of the motor that will be used in this project:

We will not go through geometry and all the theories that ancient Greeks discovered about gears. However, it is important to understand that a gear reduces the spinning speed of a motor. For example, when you ride a bicycle or drive a car, you have the choice to change the speed with the appropriate component. You actually change gears and it is easy to see that in your bicycle. A simple DC motor, like the one shown in the preceding image, follows the exact same principle.

Wheel

The wheel or wheels of your mobile robot are very important. A wheel usually consists of rubber, so as to have big rubbing force with the ground and spin without gliding at the ground. There are two qualities of rubber on the market. Usually, the cheap wheels are made of rubber that is quite hard to bend and glides a bit. The other rubber material is more *real rubber* and it is quite good for that kind or robots. It does not glide at the ground even if the material is glass or tiles. Unfortunately, there is no way to understand how good the rubber is using your eye without touching the wheel. So, keep that in mind when you buy your wheels. Both wheels described earlier have a B-shape hole and it is used to connect the wheel with the motor. You can see this in the following image:

The cheap option here is to use plastic gear motors, plastic wheels, and plastic connections. It is easy to understand that plastic things are cheaper than iron ones. So, yes they will do the work but, if you have a good budget, go for iron. An example is shown in the following image:

Obviously, you will not see a huge difference in the mobile robot's total behavior. However, it will be more stable, without so many errors or or much need to balance your motor wheels and other stuff like that, which is actually extra pain in the overall project.

Encoders

As mentioned earlier, it is important to have the speed of the motor at every single moment. Thus, we need a component which actually informs us about it. This component is called encoder. An encoder can be external or internal of the motor. An encoder is a system that knows how many RPMs a motor has turned and feeds the controller with that data. It is important to have as much detail as possible. There are encoders with 500, 1000, or 2000 and more holes in the disk and of course the higher the number of holes, the better the result and fewer the system errors. An encoder is that black disk mounted on the other side of the motor as you can see in the following image:

As the motor turns, the disk turns and the only thing that is missing is a system that is able to understand how many holes passed from a starting point. That system is the encoder chip, which is shown in the following figure and we will shortly see how it works:

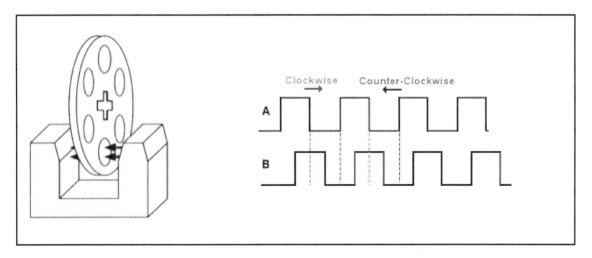

A light beam is transferred from the one side to another as the arrows show. The right edge is the transmitter of the light beam and the left is the receiver. You obviously understand that only when there is a hole passing between them the receiver is able to receive the beam. As a result, we end up with something like the pulse at the right side of the preceding figure. The receiver receives HIGH and LOW signals. This is how an encoder works and at the programming section of the chapter, we will see how to convert that 0 and 1 to something more useful. The following image shows a motor with internal encoder:

By now we have covered enough DC motors and how the actuators work. Next, we will cover the hardware that we need to build a simple two-wheeled mobile robot. We will go through every component and describe what is it and how it works.

Hardware overview

In this section, we will cover all the necessary hardware. Upcoming is a list of all the hardware used. Of course, you can use anything else you want instead of the ones mentioned here, but I think that the list is cheap enough to build your first robot. To sum up, we will build a two-wheeled robot with encoders, using Arduino Mega as the controller board and lastly a Bluetooth to have a connection with our Android application:

- DC motor and wheels
- Motor encoders
- Arduino microcontroller
- Motor shield
- Servo
- Ultrasonic distance sensor
- Bluetooth

- Breadboard
- Battery
- Other components

The final robot that we will make is as follows:

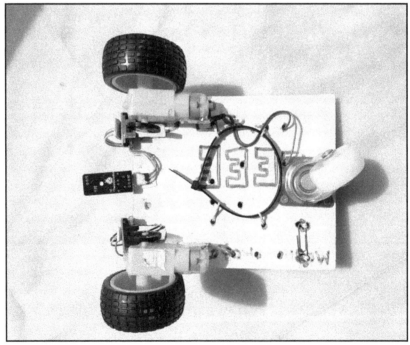

DC motor and wheels

As we have already described, the DC motor is an actuator, the component that will produce the vehicle speed. We will use simple DC motors that are quite cheap and easily found on the market. The DC motors used are controlled from 3V to 11V and they look like this:

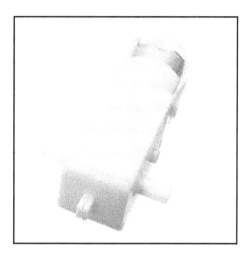

They have an axis in which one side is for the wheel and the other for the encoder. If you find motors with already soldered pins, prefer them because the motor pins can easily be damaged. We will need two DC motors, as shown in the preceding image.

Next, the wheels used for this project are as follows; they come with a Dupont male plug:

The wheel diameter is 66 mm * 26 mm. We will need one wheel for each motor.

Encoder

Next, the encoder that we will use is quite common and can be found at the following link:
`http://www.ebay.com/itm/Wheel-Encoder-Kit-For-Robot-Car-/221245494078?hash=item`
`338342533e`. The encoder comes with a disk and a chip, which does the job with the light
beam explained earlier.

Next, you can see the part of the encoder that actually spins are the wheel spin and let the
light beam reach its destination through the holes. Expensive robots have more than 2000
holes but, as said, they are really expensive:

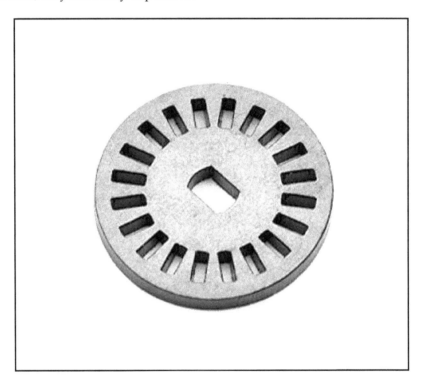

Next you can see the electronic part of the encoder. This black plastic contains a sensor that activates a beam from the one edge to the other. If there is a hole between the beam, it reaches its destination and we call it as HIGH or 1 and if something is between we call it as LOW or 0. As the mobile robot moves, we have many 0 and 1 and this is a pulse:

Arduino microcontroller

The next component that we need is the Arduino microcontroller. Usually, people use Arduino UNO for this kind of project, but we will use Arduino Mega because later on we need to use our Ultrasonic distance sensor and other sensors as well. So find your Arduino Mega either from http://www.ebay.com/ or any other store you prefer.

Your Arduino should look like this:

Motorshield

Since Arduino Mega is working on 5V, it cannot control our motors and produce their max speed. Thus, we need a shield named *Motor shield by Adafruit* that we will plug it over our Arduino and use its libraries to control the motors, as we will see in the programming topic of this chapter. The shield that we will use is as follows:

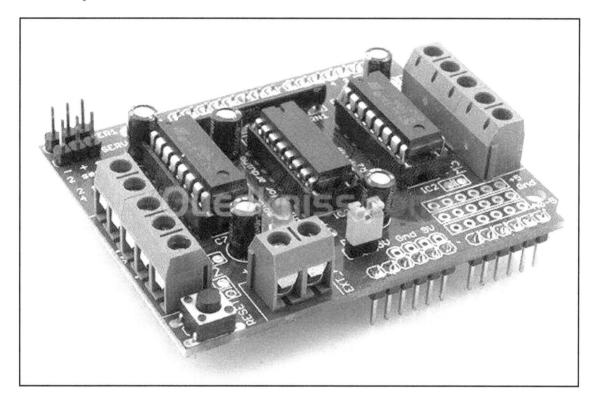

It can control up to 4 DC motors and two servos if needed. For this project, we will control two DC motors, and the servo will be controlled directly from the Arduino mega board.

Servo

A servo mechanism is something like a motor, but instead of turning around it can turn only 180 degrees. Imagine this mechanism as a system that turns from 0 to 180 degrees and then back to 0. It has also the capability to stay at a specific angle, where a simple DC motor cannot stop, it keeps spinning until we cut the power. A simple servo like the one that we will use in our project is shown in the following screenshot:

It has three wires, the first one is for the 5V input power, the second one is for the ground, and the last one is for the signal, which determines the position of the servo. The following code turns the servo from 0 to 180 degrees and back to 0. To use the following code with the Arduino microcontroller, we need a library called `Servo.h`.

Firstly, we have need to include the library in our sketch:

```
#include <Servo.h>
```

Then, define a `Servo` variable:

```
Servo myServo;
```

And then, in the `setup()` function, initiate the servo and define the pin to which our servo is attached. We can do this with the following code:

```
myServo.attach(4); // We assume that we attached the servo in the 4 digital
ping
```

Then, in the `loop()` function, we have to turn the servo from 0 to 180 and back to 0. To do this, we will use a for loop and write every position from 0 to 180:

```
for(int i=0; i<180; i++) {
    myServo.write(i);
}
for(int i=180; i>0; i--) {
    myServo.write(i);
}
```

Ultrasonic sensor

We have used an ultrasonic distance sensor to measure the distance between the mobile robot and all of the objects in a range of 180 degrees in front of the robot. The ultrasonic sensor is used with a servo mechanism as described next that helps scan a bigger area. The sensor used is shown in the following screenshot:

As you can see, it has two circles that we call the trig circle and the echo circle respectively. The trig circle throws the ultrasonic beam and, as soon as it hits in any solid object, it returns and is captured from the echo circle. We will not go through the details and the geometry of this process. However, it is important to understand that there is a duration in which the ultrasonic sound travels from the sensors and returns. This duration is divided by a number and we can get the distance of the object. Next, you will find the code that we need for all this process using an Arduino controller.

At first, we have to define the pins that the trig and echo pin is connected to. Let's assume that we have connected the echo pin to the Arduino digital `pin 7` and the trig pin to the Arduino `pin 8`:

```
#define echoPin 7 // Echo Pin
#define trigPin 8 // Trigger Pin
```

In the `setup()` function, we have to define what kind of pins they are. So, we define the trig pin as an output pin and the echo pin as our input. The reason for this is simple. The trig pin, as explained earlier, sends an ultrasonic sound from the sensor to the environment; so, it is an output, where the echo received (or not) the sound, so we can call it our input:

```
pinMode(trigPin, OUTPUT);
pinMode(echoPin, INPUT);
```

In the loop, you can create a function named `getDistance()` and add the following implementation. We have to create a pulse with two second `LOW` and then `HIGH` for 10 seconds. With that pulse, we can grab the duration and if we divide that with 58.2 we can get the distance from the ultrasonic sensor to the closest object found or null if there is nothing in front:

```
digitalWrite(trigPin, LOW);
delayMicroseconds(2);
digitalWrite(trigPin, HIGH);
delayMicroseconds(10);
digitalWrite(trigPin, LOW);
duration = pulseIn(echoPin, HIGH);

//Calculate the distance (in cm) based on the speed of sound.
distance = duration/58.2;
```

Lastly, in your function, you can either have a global variable with the name of distance or return the distance with the following line of code:

```
return distance;
```

Now, you should have a function that it is working perfectly with your sonar and gets the distance. Next, you will find the full code to test your connections. You might need to change the pins defined in the initial lines:

```
#define echoPin 24 // Echo Pin
#define trigPin 26 // Trigger Pin
#define LEDPin 13 // Onboard LED

int maximumRange = 200; // Maximum range needed
int minimumRange = 0; // Minimum range needed
long duration, distance; // Duration used to calculate distance

 void setup() {
  Serial.begin (9600);
  pinMode(trigPin, OUTPUT);
  pinMode(echoPin, INPUT);
  pinMode(LEDPin, OUTPUT); // Use LED indicator (if required)
 }

 void loop() {
 /* The following trigPin/echoPin cycle is used to determine the
  distance of the nearest object by bouncing soundwaves off of it. */
  digitalWrite(trigPin, LOW);
  delayMicroseconds(2);

  digitalWrite(trigPin, HIGH);
  delayMicroseconds(10);

  digitalWrite(trigPin, LOW);
  duration = pulseIn(echoPin, HIGH);

  //Calculate the distance (in cm) based on the speed of sound.
  distance = duration/58.2;

  if (distance >= maximumRange || distance <= minimumRange){
  /* Send a negative number to computer and Turn LED ON
  to indicate "out of range" */
  Serial.println("-1");
  digitalWrite(LEDPin, HIGH);
  }
  else {
  /* Send the distance to the computer using Serial protocol, and
  turn LED OFF to indicate successful reading. */
  Serial.println(distance);
  digitalWrite(LEDPin, LOW);
  }

  //Delay 50ms before next reading.
```

```
    delay(50);
}
```

Bluetooth

A Bluetooth sensor is a device that communicates with the TX/RX pins of the Arduino and, of course, it receives data using the Bluetooth communication protocol. Counter to all the previous sensors. it is extremely easy to be burned by simply connecting the wrong wires. The Bluetooth sensor that we will be using is called **HC06** and it looks like this:

It usually consists of six pins, but we use only four of them. If you look closer to the pinout, you will see that the actual pins (the pins to the edges are not used) are 3.3V, GND, TX, and RX. Notice that if you connect the GND to the power of the Arduino it will instantly burn and there is no way back. Also, if for any reason the 5V pin or the GND pin touches an area of the Arduino that must not touch, it may also burn. So, place it as far as possible from the Arduino, do not test the pinout connections, and, if possible, plug it to a breadboard so that it will be safe. Obviously, the power is a 3.3V or 5V. The following screenshot shows how to connect the Bluetooth module with your Arduino:

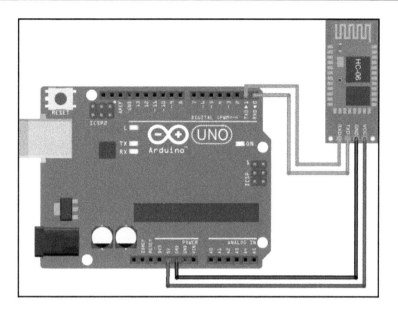

For those who wonder why should you use a Bluetooth module with the Arduino and not just use the Bluetooth of the Raspberry Pi board, well if you use the Bluetooth of the Raspberry Pi board, then you will not be able to fully use the default pins.

The following code can be used to test your connections; you can read from the Arduino what the serial receives:

```
#include <SoftwareSerial.h>

SoftwareSerial mySerial(0,1);
String Data = "";

void setup()
{
    Serial.begin(9600);
    mySerial.begin(9600);
    //Serial.println("Hello world");
}

void loop() // run over and over
{
    while (mySerial.available() > 0)
    {
        //Serial.println("Something is available");
        char character = mySerial.read(); // Receive a single character
from the software serial port
        Data.concat(character); // Add the received character to the
```

```
receive buffer

        if (character == '\n')
        {
            //Serial.print("Received: ");
            Serial.println(Data);

            // Add your code to parse the received line here....

            // Clear receive buffer so we're ready to receive the next
line
            Data = "";
        }
    }
  }
```

Breadboard

The breadboard is a simple component that allows us to debug your robot and connect more sensors. The alternative way is to solder wires but I prefer to plug them, connect them to the controller, and then test the robot. As soon as I reach my final robot, then I remove it and solder everything together. A simple breadboard is as shown in the following screenshot:

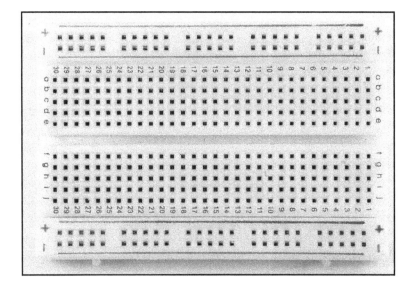

Battery

Since we are building a mobile robot, we have many choices here. We can use LiPo or Nihm or even NIcD batteries. The advantage of a LiPo battery over the other technologies is its weight. This is the reason that someone chose this kind of battery also. Weight is a crucial factor of the overall project since it affects the duration of the movement. A LiPo battery is defined from the following:

- Capacity (mah)
- Voltages (V)
- Cells

The capacity is how much energy the battery can store. Imagine this as the amount of water in a bottle. Furthermore, the higher the voltage, the more torque a DC motor can have. The battery depends on your application. For the sake of simplicity, we will choose a common battery pack as shown in the following image:

Notice that it is important to connect all our batteries in the right order. There are two ways of a connecting a battery, the serial way and the parallel way. When connecting batteries in the serial way, you increase the total voltage of the battery pack to the sum of each battery voltage. On the other hand, when connecting in the parallel way, you have the same voltage as each battery has, but you increase the milliampere per hour (mAh). That way you increase the capacity of the battery with the same voltages. For this project, we will connect our batteries in the serial way and increase the voltage up to 7.5. Each battery has 1.5 voltage, so if we connect five batteries in a series, we add the voltage. So 1.5 * 5 = 7.5 V.

Other components

We have already seen some major components of our mobile robot. Of course you can use yours and everything else that you might already have from the previous projects. We can always add a camera module in our mobile and have *eyes*. Many similar projects add three distance sensors or an MPU 6050 that is actually an IMU. MPU6050 has three gyroscopes and three accelerometers. That provides us some more information. The following is an image of a MPU6050 sensor:

Motor soldering

We saw some basic components of a two-wheel mobile robot. They are the fundamentals of robotics and almost every robot has some of them. In this section, we will go through all the necessary actions you have to do to assemble all the previous components into a working mobile robot.

In the following image, you can see some helpful tools that can make your soldering easier. Obviously, always prefer a soldering station, but the following should do the job. After all, we only have to solder the motors:

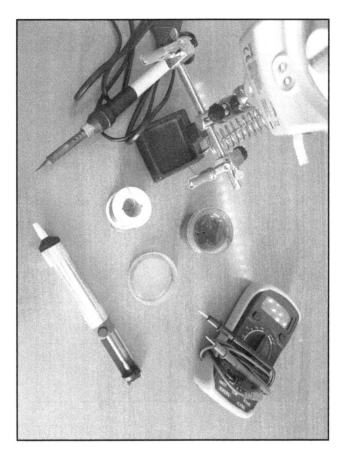

The multimeter is useful for measuring the voltages from the motors and sometimes debug our robot. A not-so-good soldering connection may have the result of lower voltage and thus lower RPM in the motor.

Place the soldering iron on the motor and connect the wires. Keeping the soldering iron over the wires for more than 10 seconds may cause the plastic cover of the motor to melt. Of course, that depends on your soldering iron or your soldering station. The result with a good soldering connection should be something like this:

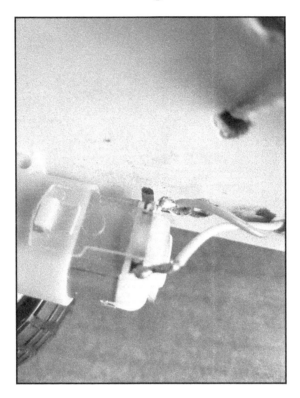

Programming the controller

The microcontroller is an Arduino UNO R3 and our Raspberry Pi Zero W. The motors and the distance sensor will be controlled using an Arduino microcontroller. Then the microcontroller will be communicating with the Raspberry Pi Zero W board. Depending on the motor shield you will be using, you may need to change some part of the code but the main idea is the same. As mentioned in the hardware overview section, the motor shield that we will be using requires a specific library. The first thing that we have to do is download the library from Github and save the files in the appropriate folder. You can find the library at the following link:

AFMotor library: `https://github.com/adafruit/Adafruit-Motor-Shield-library`

After downloading all the necessary files, you need to place them under `homefolder` | `Arduino` | `libraries` and extract the file. Then, open your Arduino IDE, go to **File** | **Examples**, and find the new library installed. There are some examples there and you can easily use them to test your motors. Assuming that you have made some tests, we are now going to write the full controller.

Basic concept

The basic idea is to develop a controller using our Arduino and the motor shield to control the two motors. There are several ways to do that. This means that you can use your Android device with an app to control its motion and movement. You can also use nothing and make it fully autonomous. Lastly, there is the option to control it through a computer using Wi-Fi. In this chapter, we will see the autonomous mobile robot and go through a way of how you can setup your connection with a computer using the Raspberry Pi Zero W board.

The code consists of three main parts. The first one is the code that creates the necessary variables and constants, the second part is the setup function of the Arduino that initializes the variables used in the part 1, and the last one, part 3, is the main loop. Part 3 is actually the controller.

Controller development

The following code is an example of how you can work and create your own controller. We will be using AFMotor, Servo, and math libraries:

```
#include <AFMotor.h>
#include <Servo.h>
#include <math.h>
```

At first, we need to define all the pins we will be using. Notice that you can change them and define yours. In the following example, you must use Arduino Mega:

```
#define echoPin 24 // Echo Pin
#define trigPin 26 // Trigger Pin
#define LEDPin 13 // Onboard LED
#define objAvoidPin 22
#define leftEncPin 40
#define rightEncPin 43

AF_DCMotor leftMotor(4);  // M4 - LEFT motor
AF_DCMotor rightMotor(2);  // M2 - RIGHT motor
```

```
... and more
```

At this point, you need to initialize some variables. Define each pin, whether it is INPUT or OUTPUT:

```
void setup() {
   Serial.begin(9600);              // set up Serial library at 9600 bps
   Serial.println("Mobile robot up and ready...");
   pinMode(objAvoidPin, INPUT);

   pinMode(trigPin, OUTPUT);
   pinMode(echoPin, INPUT);
   delay(3000);
}
```

At this point, you need to create some functions to make your coding easier. For example, you can see some of them in the following code and understand that we need a function to get the distance of the front Ultrasonic sensor. Another one, to move forward, move backward, turn left and right.

The updateFrontDistance function reads the ultrasonic distance sensor and stores the result at a global variable. The following functions spin the motor forward or backward:

```
void moveForward(){
  Serial.println("\tMoving forward...");
  leftMotor.run(FORWARD);
  rightMotor.run(FORWARD);

  leftMotor.setSpeed(180);
  rightMotor.setSpeed(180);
}

void posStop(){
  Serial.println("\tStoping...");
  leftMotor.run(RELEASE);
  rightMotor.run(RELEASE);
}

void moveLeft(){
  Serial.print("moving left");
  leftMotor.setSpeed(0);
  rightMotor.setSpeed(150);
  delay(1200);
  rightMotor.setSpeed(0);
}

void turnRight(){
```

```
    Serial.println("\tTurning right...");
    leftMotor.setSpeed(200);
    rightMotor.setSpeed(0);
  }

  // Turns the servo 180 degrees and finds the position that the mobile can
go forward
  void findEmptyRoute() {

    for(int i=10; i<160; i++) {
      Serial.println("Increasing servo ");
      servo.write(i);
        if(distance <=25) {
          updateFrontDistance();
          Serial.print("Distance: ");
          Serial.println(distance);
        }

    }
  }
```

The `FDSController` function is used to detect an object and turn the mobile robot:

```
void FDSController() {
    if ( (distance >= 35) && (distance <= 100)) {  // Object detected
      moveForward();
      delay(1000);
    }else {
      turnRight();
      delay(500);
    }
}
```

Lastly, in the loop function, you can uncomment the part of code depending on your goal. Now, the controller is checking the distance of the front sensor and moves forward or turns right if an object is found.

More information can be found in the github repository.

Now, it is time to use our Raspberry Pi Zero W board to connect our Arduino with a device. You can do that using the Bluetooth module or even Wi-Fi. For example, one way is to set up a webpage with four buttons and connect to the webpage using your mobile phone or a computer. When clicking on a button, you will be able to send serial data from the Raspberry Pi to your Arduino.

Another way of communicating is using only the Bluetooth module and an Android application. With the Android application, you can control the movement of the mobile robot. Move to the front or back or turn to the right or left. There are various apps in the PlayStore and if you have some knowledge about Android development, you can always create your own.

When developing a controller, there are two things that matter. First of all, you have to decide what messages you will send from the controller to your Raspberry Pi board and then what messages you will send from the Raspberry Pi board to your Arduino controller. In your Raspberry Pi board, you can start a serial communication with your Arduino board using the Serial library. Type Python to open the shell:

```
python
```

Then import the serial library by typing the following:

```
import Serial
```

Then, create a serial communication with your Arduino by typing the following:

```
ser = serial.Serial(port, baudrate);
```

Here the port is the port in which your Arduino is connected and the baud rate is up to you. Usually, the default `baudrate` is `9600`. Remember that in Linux the port is something like `/dev/tty***`, whereas, in Windows it is something like `COM*`. By replacing these you can start the communication and now you should be able to talk from your Raspberry to your Arduino board.

Future ideas

This project was about building a two-wheel mobile robot. The logic and basic knowledge behind this is crucial for building any similar robot. We can add components and chips in the mobile robot and make it better with more functionalities.

Four motor mobile robots

You can easily modify the robot by adding two more motors and two more wheels. Then, your mobile robot will be four motor driven. Obviously, you need to modify the code and add what is necessary, but this should not be a problem since the core is already coded. When changing the way that a mobile robot moves, we need to think what things this change affects. This means that the center of mass may be changed and the orbit of a movement may be different. For example, the following is a four-wheeled mobile robot:

As far as the wheels and motors are concerned, you can perform another simple change. Add crawlers to your robot and make it able to move over dust or muddy terrain. Next, you can see that crawlers are quite useful for those kind of terrains, but of course they are quite expensive, where simple wheels may cost just $ 2:

Furthermore, you can add a Grapple with an arm to hold it. A grapple is an awesome way to grab things and move them or change their position. There are several projects using a Grapple like the robot you can see in the following image. Usually, the Grapple is controlled by a servo mechanism, but not so cheap as used for the ultrasonic distance sensor in this project. It is usually servo with metallic gears that can handle more pressure and produce more torque:

It may be a good idea to start a new project and learn how to control a Grapple with an arm before adding it to your mobile robot. That way you can be sure that your external Grapple add-on is working properly. It is an easier way to debug your future problems.

As far as the sensors are concerned, there are several solutions, depending on what you want to do. Many developers have added a camera to the Raspberry Pi board and use algorithms to track a moving object, other moving mobiles, identify a user, or even fully control the robot using **Image Based Visual Servoing** (**IBVS**). More information about these advance topics can be found in Google search as always. It is important and very helpful if you have some basic knowledge and read relevant papers.

A robot using the camera mentioned earlier can be found in the following image:

There are no limitations on what you can do with a mobile robot. The only limitation is in your fantasy, so do some google search, watch some videos in YouTube, and think what you want to do. It may have be done already by someone.

Summary

In this chapter, we went through the fundamentals of robotics and of course the development of a simple mobile robot. It may seem quite easy to create a mobile robot like this, but, for example, an autonomous vacuum cleaner is not so different. You just need to solve one more project there, which has nothing to do with the robot navigation. Hopefully, with this knowledge you can create your own advanced mobile robot.

In the following chapter, we will see how we can create a home bot and have an interaction with our home.

5
Home Bot

In the previous chapter, we have seen, step by step, how we can easily create a simple two-wheeled mobile robot. Further development can be done by implementing a home bot. Thus, your mobile robot will be able to communicate with your home bot and execute some scheduled tasks. So, in this chapter, we will see how we can build and develop an automated home bot assistant. Home bots are quite popular nowadays, since they automate things and actions in our home, a place where we spend the most time of our lives. The scenario that we will implement in this chapter is simple. Our Raspberry Pi Zero W will be connected to a sensor and it will send a notification back to our mobile phone if something occurs. We will cover a list of different topics, as follows:

- Introduction to home bots
- Socket programming
- Home automation

Introduction to home bots

Nowadays, bots are quite popular, and they are really useful in some cases; for example, as we have seen in `Chapter 3`, *Chatbot* a customer service representative can be completely replaced by a chatbot. As far as home is concerned, many companies, such as LG, have developed autonomous vacuum cleaners; others have developed smart refrigerators.

There are many ideas and implementations that tend to automate our lives and increase the quality of them. The following is an image of an autonomous vacuum cleaner developed by LG:

Next, we will go through socket programming, to see some examples of how we can easily communicate with our server. After that, we will implement a server and client with Slack API and other libraries.

Socket programming

Every device connected to the internet uses sockets to communicate with another device or server. The basic idea is quite simple; a client that usually has some requests connects to a server that is able to handle those kind of requests, and the communication between those two is established using sockets. Nowadays, there are many frameworks out there with which you can easily set up a communication channel, but to understand this scenario as much as we can, we will go through socket programming, and I will explain everything. To sum up, the client requests some data from the server and the server responds with an answer back to the client.

The following is a simple image representing this communication scenario:

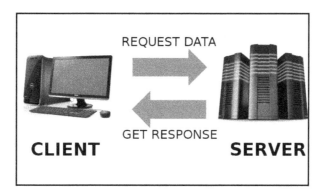

Socket programming is actually the two arrows in the preceding image. It shows how the communication is implemented and how a client can identify the server and send some data to finally get a response.

We will use Python as our programming language. If you are not familiar with it, take some time and take an online course, since it is crucial to understand some basics of programming. Python is a simple language with many available frameworks. However, we will analyze the real programming that happens under the framework. This way, you will be able to expand this project, learn more, have an overall idea of what we are doing, and debug your problems.

Simple client-server communication

Note that this communication part will work just fine, but you may need to use some libraries and not pure code, such as the simple server and client as described next. However, it is crucial to understand what is going on under the API calls. The client-server scenario happens every day. Imagine, if you go to a customer service shop and ask a question, obviously the employee will respond with an answer or a question, and then, you will say something similar to *thank you* or rephrase your question. A client (you) requests some data from a server (https://www.facebook.com or an employee) and then, the server checks whether the data is available and whether you are authorized to get the data. If no error occurs, it responds to you with your requested data, and you receive some bytes from the server. Since the server wants to be reliable, it waits for your acknowledgment with a message that says *Hello! I am the client, and I received your data. Thank you.* After this, the connection closes.

Simple server

A simple server consists of an IP address and a port. An IP address is something similar to 38.24.64.23, in which there are four parts; each one of them has a number from 1 to 254. It is similar to the address of your home, but instead of letters, we have four sets of numbers. The port can be any number between 0 to 65535. Some of them are default ports in an application; for example, when you surf the internet, you use port 80; when you SSH to a remote server (or your Pi), you use port 22. Thus, for a simple server implementation, we will use an IP address and a port. This combination defines a server uniquely all over the world. In the following example, we will use our localhost machine for the demo. So, instead of an IP address, we will use 127.0.0.1 or the name localhost, which means that the client and server are located on the same machine. You can also follow up this tutorial using these settings. Let's pick a number for our port. It is always advised to pick a number far away from 0 to 100 since there are many default ports there. So, we will use the number 8000 for our port. The server will run with the following settings:

```
IP address: 127.0.0.1 (or localhost)
Port number: 8000
```

Next, we need to set up a server and get it running. We can do this using a very easy Python code. We can either use an HTTP server from Python libraries or pure socket programming. You can find more information on the HTTP server library at https://docs.python.org/2/library/simplehttpserver.html.

With the following code, we can start an HTTP server in the current directory:

```
import SimpleHTTPServer
import SocketServer

PORT = 8000
Handler = SimpleHTTPServer.SimpleHTTPRequestHandler
httpd = SocketServer.TCPServer(("", PORT), Handler)

print "serving at port", PORT
httpd.serve_forever()
```

On the other hand, we can easily start an HTTP server with one line of code:

```
python -m SimpleHTTPServer 8000
```

If you open a browser and type `localhost` or `127.0.0.1`, you will see the result. It should look as follows:

Directory listing for /

- .adobe/
- .android/
- .AndroidStudio2.3/
- .aptitude/
- .arduino/
- .arduino-create/
- .arduino15/
- .atom/
- .audacity-data/
- .bash_history
- .bash_logout
- .bashrc
- .bashrc-anaconda2.bak
- .cache/
- .cassandra/

This list contains some of my home folder directories. Your server will depend on the directory from which you start the HTTP server. Change your current directory, and test this again. Now, the hardcore programming starts. Things were easy with libraries, such as `httpsimpleserver`, that Python provided. We will use Python again, but we will create a new server application. Open a new file with your favorite editor, and let's start writing some code. First, import the necessary libraries:

```
import socket
import time
```

Then, create a new socket with the following lines of code. Next, we have used port `8888`, so change it to whatever you want, or leave it like this for the sake of this demo. The listen method actually defines the maximum number of connections. As you can see next, in the following lines, we allow only up to five simultaneous connections. It is important to scale up your server since we obviously won't have a rack or a server room. A regular computer cannot handle thousands of connections.

```
# Create socket
sock = socket.socket(socket.AF_INET, socket.SOCK_STREAM)
sock.bind(('', 8888))
sock.listen(5)
```

Next, we will try to read the message from the client. The `accept()` method freezes forever until a new connection appears:

```
try:
    # Echo loop
    while True:
        try:
            newSocket, address = sock.accept()
except socket.error, (value, message):
            print "Socket error while waiting to accept socket: " +
message
        except:
            print "Unexpected error while waiting to accept"
            break
```

Next, the `recv()` method receives all data that the client sends. If everything goes OK then, the server responds with the message `I received your data. All ok!`

```
try:
    # Echo loop
    while True:
        try:
            newSocket, address = sock.accept()
        except socket.error, (value, message):
            print "Socket error while waiting to accept socket: " +
message
        except:
            print "Unexpected error while waiting to accept"
            break
        print "Connected from echo client ", address
        while True:
            try:
                receivedData = newSocket.recv(1024)
            except socket.error as (value, message):
                print "Socket error while waiting to receive:
(value:", value, ") " + message
                break
            except:
                print "Unexpected error while waiting to receive"
                break

            if not receivedData:
                break
            else:
                print "Server received: " + receivedData

            newSocket.sendall("I received your data. All ok!")
```

```
            # Done transacting with client
            newSocket.close()
            print "Disconnected from", address

    except:
        print "Unexpected error in echo loop"
    finally:
        sock.close()
```

In the end, we have to close the connection, since problems may occur with the open connection when trying to execute it again. It is a good programming technique to close what we don't need anymore.

Simple client

We have to develop a client application that will be much simpler. The following code will create a client that connects to an existing server and sends a message. After this, the client receives the response from the server and prints it. As a client, we can also have our mobile phone slack application, as I will describe in the advanced client later. It is important because the client-server communication requires both parts to be able to send and receive data.

At first, we have to import all the necessary libraries, as always:

```
import socket
import time
```

Next, we have to connect to the server located at the localhost:

```
sock = socket.socket(socket.AF_INET, socket.SOCK_STREAM)
sock.connect(('localhost', 8888))
print "Connected to echo server"
```

Next, we send the message to the server:

```
try:
    sock.sendall("Hello there!")
```

Now, we try to get a response or an error:

```
try:
        response = sock.recv(1024)
    except socket.error as (value, message):
        print "Socket error while waiting to receive: (value:", value, ") "
+ message
    except:
        print "Unexpected error"
```

After this, we simply print the response:

```
print "Received:", response
    if not response:
        break
    else:
        print "Message sended!"
```

Before running the client, you have to run the server code. You should make sure the server is up and then try and execute the client software. The full code is as follows:

```
import time
import socket

sock = socket.socket(socket.AF_INET, socket.SOCK_STREAM)
sock.connect(('localhost', 8888))
print "Connected to echo server"
try:
    sock.sendall("Hello there!")
    try:
        response = sock.recv(1024)
    except socket.error as (value, message):
        print "Socket error while waiting to receive: (value:", value, ") "
+ message
    except:
        print "Unexpected error"
    print "Received:", response
    if not response:
        break
    else:
        print "Message sended!"
except:
    print "Unexpected error in echo loop"

sock.close()
```

Advanced client-server communication

After a simple client-server communication, it is time to use some API calls and other libraries to develop more simple and easy-to-use communication between our server and client application. Let's start with the server implementation next. Firstly, we will implement the server side that will be our Raspberry Pi Zero W board.

Advanced server

Now, we will use the API of a service of your choice to get our notifications. There are several ways to do this, but for the sake of simplicity, we will demonstrate slack API. Slack API provides us with functions and handlers to easily alert our desktop or mobile application. It also provides a function to allow various interactions, such as sending messages back to our server and back to our home. The code that we will use is straightforward and we will not go very deep to analyze how and why it is working. Of course, the first step here is to create a slack account. Go to the official website of slack, `https://slack.com/`, to create a new team and download and install the slack application in your mobile phone as well. When we are all set, we will use Python again to write some more lines of code and connect our software with the slack application in our desktop PC or mobile. To get started, create a new folder with the name `slackapi`:

```
mkdir slackapi
```

Now, create a new `virtualenv` to isolate your application dependencies from other projects you're may be working on:

```
virtualenv venv
```

Notice that the previous step is not necessary if you know what are you doing and you want to set this up in your system. After this, you need to activate the `virtualenv` with the following code:

```
source venv/bin/activate
```

If everything goes well, you should see your prompt change to something similar to `(venv) $`, but it may also be different. You have many choices, since there are many libraries in Python, but, for simplicity, we will use `slackclient`. So, install this client with the following code:

```
pip install slackclient==1.0.0
```

Next, go to the official website of slack at `https://api.slack.com/web` and, if you are not logged in, log in with your account. Next, scroll down on the web API page, where you'll see a button to generate test tokens:

FUNDAMENTALS
Formatting Messages
Message Attachments
Unfurling links
User Presence
Rate Limits

KEEP IN TOUCH
Recent updates
Support and Discussion
@SlackAPI
Platform Blog
Slack Engineering Blog

Authentication

Authenticate your Web API requests by providing a bearer token, which identifies a single user.

Register your application with Slack to obtain credentials for use with our OAuth 2.0 implementation, which allows you to negotiate tokens on behalf of users and teams. Tokens should be passed in all Web API calls as a parameter called `token`.

While developing or testing your app, you may use test tokens using our test token generator.

Generate test tokens

⚠ Test tokens are just for you. Treat them as you would a password. Never share test tokens with other users or applications.

Notice that you must have administrative privileges to generate a test token for your slack team. If you do, generate a token. This token will serve fine for this example. For more information and advanced usage, have a look at `https://api.slack.com/custom-integrations/legacy-tokens`, where other users can generate tokens for authentication through their own accounts.

Without closing the tab, switch into your Python environment to set up and try out the API. Start the Python shell with the following code:

```
(venv) $ python
```

Test your API token with a test call by typing the following code:

```
>>> from slackclient import SlackClient
>>> slack_client = SlackClient('your test token here')
>>> slack_client.api_call("api.tet")
```

If everything goes well, you should get something similar to the following result:

```
{u'ok': False, u'error': u'invalid_auth'}
```

Check again that you copied the token correctly. For more tests, execute the following line of code as many times as you want:

```
>> slack_client.api_call("auth.test")
```

You must always get a similar response to the previous with different numbers. At this point, everything is connected via slack API and we can not obtain slack data and handle messages! Export your slack token with the following code:

```
export SLACK_TOKEN='your slack token pasted here'
```

At this point, use your favorite editor, such as vim, nano, gedit, or anything else to write some Python code. Create a new file named app.py and import the following libraries:

```
import os
 from slackclient import SlackClient
```

After this, get the token that you have previously exported to the OS and create a slack client as we did in our previous example:

```
SLACK_TOKEN = os.environ.get('SLACK_TOKEN')
 slack_client = SlackClient(SLACK_TOKEN)
```

Now, let's create a new function to list channels via an API call. Slack returns the results in a dictionary with two keys: ok and channels.list. The first one, ok, allows us to know if the API call was successful or not, and thus, if its value is true, then channels will contain all the data we need. In case we have no channel, it will return false.

```
def list_channels():
    channels_call = slack_client.api_call("channels.list")
    if channels_call.get('ok'):
        return channels_call['channels']
    return None
```

Finally, add your main function that will allow us to print all the channels:

```
if __name__ == '__main__':
    channels = list_channels()
    if channels:
        print("Channels: ")
        for c in channels:
            print(c['name'] + " (" + c['id'] + ")")
    else:
        print("Unable to authenticate.")
```

This is pretty much all the code we need. Save your file and execute the script from the command line with the following code:

```
python app.py
```

You will get an output similar to the following:

```
Channels:
 general (C0S82S5RS)
 python (C0S8HABL3)
 random (C0S8F4432)
```

Notice that slack's API needs a unique reference for channels. This means that we can easily use the ID and not the name to reference a channel. At this point, you should understand what we are trying to do. Our next and final step here is to send some data back to the application using different slack API methods. You can combine all the code that was demonstrated to develop your own software.

The updated code is as follows:

```python
import os
 from slackclient import SlackClient

 SLACK_TOKEN = os.environ.get('SLACK_TOKEN', None)
 slack_client = SlackClient(SLACK_TOKEN)

def list_channels():
    channels_call = slack_client.api_call("channels.list")
    if channels_call['ok']:
        return channels_call['channels']
    return None

def channel_info(channel_id):
    channel_info = slack_client.api_call("channels.info",
channel=channel_id)
    if channel_info:
        return channel_info['channel']
    return None

  if __name__ == '__main__':
    channels = list_channels()
    if channels:
        print("Channels: ")
        for c in channels:
            print(c['name'] + " (" + c['id'] + ")")
            detailed_info = channel_info(c['id'])
            if detailed_info:
                print(detailed_info['latest']['text'])
    else:
        print("Unable to authenticate.")
```

To send messages back to slack via API calls, we have to add a new method, as follows:

```
def send_message(channel_id, message):
    slack_client.api_call(
        "chat.postMessage",
        channel=channel_id,
        text=message,
        username='pythonbot',
        icon_emoji=':robot_face:'
    )
```

This way, we can send messages to the `#general` channel. Your main function should look as follows:

```
if __name__ == '__main__':
    channels = list_channels()
    if channels:
        print("Channels: ")
        for channel in channels:
            print(channel['name'] + " (" + channel['id'] + ")")
            detailed_info = channel_info(channel['id'])
            if detailed_info:
                print('Latest text from ' + channel['name'] + ":")
                print(detailed_info['latest']['text'])
            if channel['name'] == 'general':
                send_message(channel['id'], "Hello " +
                            channel['name'] + "! It worked!")
        print('-----')
    else:
        print("Unable to authenticate.")
```

Notice that for all channels, we search for the channel that has the name `general`. Once we find this, we send a message with the channel ID and the word `Hello`, then the channel name, and then a message `! It worked!`. If you save the file and execute the code again, you should now get a notification on your slack application in the general channel. Try and change the message to something that you like, and test this out again:

At this point, you have learned how to create a notification with slack API calls. It is pretty easy to combine our previous code with the temperature sensor and the new code with the slack API, and send a notification when the temperature is over 25 degrees Celsius.

Advanced client

The client here is actually the application in our mobile device or our desktop computer. For the sake of simplicity and for this project, the client will not send any messages back to the server. The client will only receive notifications if the temperature goes over 25 degrees Celsius. However, the advanced client can be developed by adding two functions. The actual function that sends a message:

```
def send_message(channel_id, message):
    slack_client.api_call(
        "chat.postMessage",
        channel=channel_id,
        text=message,
        username='pythonbot',
        icon_emoji=':robot_face:'
    )
```

In the previous code, you choose the channel in which you want to send the message and of course the `main` function:

```
if __name__ == '__main__':
    channels = list_channels()
    if channels:
        print("Channels: ")
        for channel in channels:
            print(channel['name'] + " (" + channel['id'] + ")")
            detailed_info = channel_info(channel['id'])
            if detailed_info:
                print('Latest text from ' + channel['name'] + ":")
                print(detailed_info['latest']['text'])
            if channel['name'] == 'general':
                send_message(channel['id'], "Hello " +
                            channel['name'] + "! It worked!")
        print('-----')
    else:
        print("Unable to authenticate.")
```

We will not analyze this code, but you can try it out to send messages back to the server; for example, you can simply get a notification and send back an `ok` message.

Home automation

To complete home automation, we will use our Raspberry Pi Zero W board and a DHT11 temperature and humidity sensor. The DHT11 sensor is able to test both temperature and humidity. It is pretty easy to set it up and we will do this using a library. First of all, let's start connecting things together. The DHT11 sensor consists of only three pins, one for the ground, one for the 5V and the last one for the signal. We have to carefully connect them to the appropriate pins in our Raspberry Pi Zero W board. In the following image, you can find the pinout of the board:

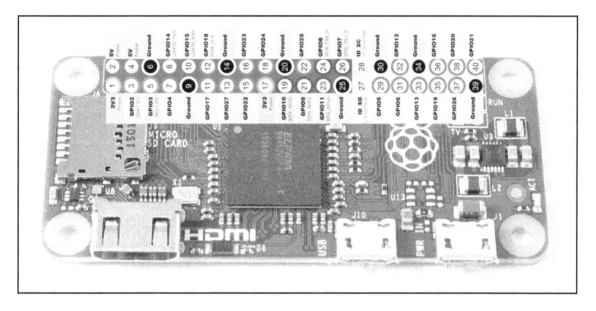

If this project is brand new and not an add-on, all pins should be available; so, connect the ground pin of the sensor to pin **9**. Next, connect the 5V pin of the sensor to pin **2**, and finally, connect the signal pin of the sensor to pin **7**. It is important to be connected to pin **7**, since we will later bind this pin with our Python code.

The following is an image of the temperature and humidity sensor that we used:

First of all, update your Pi board with the latest distribution:

```
sudo apt-get update
```

Then, if git is not installed in your Pi board, install it so that we can later clone the appropriate repository from GitHub:

```
sudo apt-get install git-core
```

Next, you have to install the Adafruit DHT11 library. We will use this library to connect our Pi sensor with the Python code and read the temperature and humidity:

```
git clone https://github.com/adafruit/Adafruit_Python_DHT.git
```

Change your current directory to the directory you just downloaded:

```
cd Adafruit_Python_DHT
```

To write our code and end this part, if you don't have them installed, install all the necessary libraries:

```
sudo apt-get install build-essential python-dev
```

Finally, install the library with the following code:

```
sudo python setup.py install
```

Now, we should be ready to run our code and output the temperature and humidity. If `vim` is not installed in your Pi run, you can skip this step and use your favorite editors, such as nano or GUI gedit:

```
sudo apt-get install vim
```

Once it is installed, open the vim editor by typing (you can also skip this step):

```
vim
```

After pressing `i` to go into insert mode, type the following code:

```
#!/usr/bin/python
import sys
import Adafruit_DHT
import time

while True:
    humidity, temperature = Adafruit_DHT.read_retry(11, 4)
    print "Humidity: " + str(humidity)
    print "Temperature: " + str(temperature) + "\n"
    time.sleep(1)
```

The code is actually pretty simple; we have created a `while` loop, which means that the block inside it will run forever; then, you call the `Adafruit_DHT.read_retry(11, 4)` function to return the humidity and temperature at pin **7** that we have attached to our sensor. Lastly, we print the data and sleep for one second.

To close and save the file, press *Esc*, then type `:wq! example.py`, and hit *Enter*. You should see a file named `example.py`. For more information, take a look at `http://vim.wikia.com/wiki/Saving_a_file`. To run the code, just type:

```
python example.py
```

You should see an output, as follows:

```
pi@raspberrypi:~/ch5-temp-project$ python temphum.py
Humidity: 91.0
Temperature: 25.0

Humidity: 91.0
Temperature: 26.0

Humidity: 91.0
Temperature: 25.0
```

Now, it should be easy to create an if statement inside the Python code, and check if the temperature is over 25 degrees Celsius, then execute and call the slack code that we have developed before. You can easily add more automation here and make your bot smarter and able to understand more things in your environment.

Summary

In this chapter, we went through the development of a socket communication client-server application. We went through some basic functions of socket programming on a very low programming level but also on higher levels, using slack API calls and simple HTTP Python libraries. You should be able to add more sensors to your Raspberry Pi Zero W board and adjust your code to automate more things and actions. Your home bot should make your house more secure and smarter! In the next chapter, we will play with cameras and face recognition.

6
Security Camera

In the previous chapter, we explored home bots. We covered how a home bot can be autonomous and send notifications back to you. In this chapter, we will go through the development of a security camera. We will demonstrate an advanced way to connect your camera to your Raspberry Pi board using MotionPie. Later, we will discuss a library named OpenCV in case you want to scale up this project. To sum up, here are the topics that we will be covering in this chapter:

- Installing a camera
- Installing MotionPie
- Configuring MotionPie settings
- Installing OpenCV
- Face recognition

Installing a camera

As with all Raspberry Pi boards, the new Raspberry Pi Zero W board has a slot for a camera connection. However, first of all, we need to buy a Raspberry Pi camera in case we do not have one. There are two types of camera that you can buy--a normal IR camera or a non-IR camera. The normal IR camera does not let you see well in dark spots. This means that as soon as the sun goes down, it will be hard to view any objects. On the other hand, non-IR cameras are great for this kind of project. Depending on the project, buy the appropriate camera. Here, you can find two links for both camera types.

The Raspberry Pi 5MP Camera Board Module can be found at the following link:
```
https://www.amazon.com/gp/product/B00E1GGE40/ref=as_li_tl?ie=
UTF8camp=1789creative=390957creativeASIN=B00E1GGE40linkCode=as2
tag=pimylifeup-20linkId=JKO72D2M4YJG3YCK
```

The normal camera looks as follows:

The Raspberry Pi 5MP 1080P Camera NoIR (no IR filter) Night Vision Module can be found at the following link:
```
https://www.amazon.com/gp/product/B00G76YEU8/ref=as_li_tl?ie=UTF
8&camp=1789&creative=390957&creativeASIN=B00G76YEU8&linkCode=as2
&tag=pimylifeup-20&linkId=3HZBGLZYYAUE4NTY
```

The advanced camera module looks as follows. It has no IR filter and is awesome for night vision purposes:

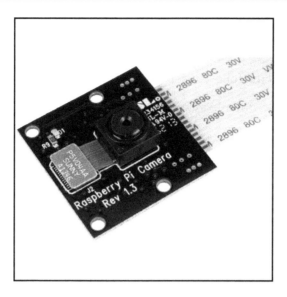

To connect your camera to your Raspberry Pi Zero W board, simply place it in by hand and pull up both sides of the connector. As soon as the connector is pulled up, try to place the ribbon cable inside and gently press the board connector that you pulled up before. Now, the camera should be locked on the board and that is it:

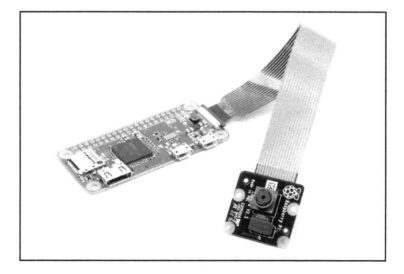

Installing MotionPie

MotionPie is a great solution for many different projects when a camera is involved. To install MotionPie, refer to the following steps:

1. First, we have to download and format our SD card with the appropriate software:

    Download the latest release from the GitHub repository and format your SD card. The link to the repository is `https://github.com/ccrisan/motioneyeos/releases`. If you do not remember how to format your SD card, further reference from `Chapter 1`, *Introduction to Raspberry Pi Zero W*, where Raspberry Pi Zero W was introduced and go through the instructions once again.

2. Next, insert your SD card and boot up your board.
3. We now need to find the IP address or hostname of the Raspberry Pi board. If you are an advanced user, skip this step else, follow the instructions:

   - For Windows users, go to the network, then file explorer, and you should see a computer name such as MP-E28D9CE5. Copy this name and open up a browser. Type the following:

     ```
     http://MP-E28D9CE5
     ```

   - Now, if everything is ok, you should have the Motion Pie interface up and running.
   - Another way to find the IP address of the Raspberry Pi board is by navigating to the router and finding out which device connected wirelessly is named *Raspberry Pi*. To log in as admin, navigate to the key symbol in the upper-left corner. Note that the username is *admin* and the password should be left blank. Of course, we will change them later, but for now, just log in. If everything goes *OK*, you will be able to see the interface of the camera and access all the settings for the camera stream.

Set up multiple network cameras

If you want to scale this up and connect more network cameras using the software, it should be pretty easy. This way, you can have more than one camera streams in just one window. To do this follow these steps:

1. Click on the three lines in the upper-left corner of the software.
2. There should appear a drop-down box in the upper-left corner; click on it and select **add camera**.

Now, we need to set up all four necessary settings:

1. First, `Device` is what allows you to select where the camera will be located and what type it is; for example, it can be located on the local network, and it can be an MJPEG camera type.
2. Next, `URL` is the URL of the other network camera. Each camera has an IP address or a hostname in the local network, for example, `http://othercamera:8080`.
3. Next, `Username` and the `Password` are fields of the camera device. For more security in your system, it is recommended to add a username and a password and not to leave it blank.
4. Lastly, the `Camera` field actually allows you to select the camera you wish to add to the system and that is it. Now, all the necessary setup is done.

With that being said, now, you can have a single window and view different camera streams.

Connecting a camera outside of your local network

At this point, you should consider connecting your Raspberry Pi Zero W board with your router and gaining access from anywhere in the world. To do this, you have to port forward the incoming connections to your Raspberry Pi Zero W board, as we have already seen in previous chapters when talking about networking. Basically, what you have to do is find your Raspberry Pi Zero W IP address and after logging in on your router interface, create a port forward rule from all or specific incoming connections to that IP address and port `80`. Next, to secure your local security camera system, you may consider to set up a username and password.

This way, you make it harder for unwanted users to access your local security system. After this, you can open up a browser and go to the <X.X.X.X>:80 URL, where X.X.X.X is your home/router IP address from your ISP. You can find this IP address by simply visiting Google and searching *What is my IP address?*. Consider changing port 80 to some other port that only you should know. This makes it harder for anyone else to access your system. They would actually need to scan your network for open ports and find which one you use. Remember that we can create as many security layers as we can, and there is no way that you can be 100% secure from anyone.

Configuring MotionPie settings

Now, it is time to configure the MotionPie settings. Assuming that you have opened MotionPie interface, you should be able to see the interface of MotionPie, as follows:

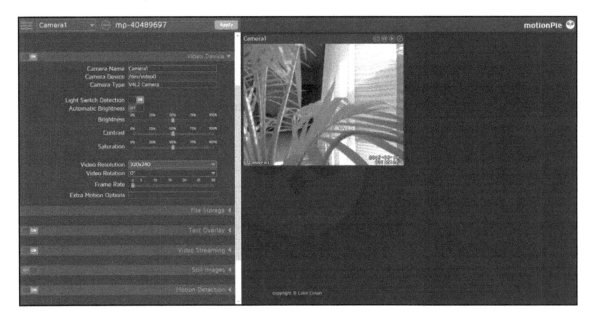

On the left of the screen, there are several sections with different settings. First, we will go through general settings.

General settings

In this section, you will be able to set the administrator username and password as we discussed earlier. This is an important step and you should not skip it. This account will have access to all the settings you're seeing at the moment. Surveillance username and password can also be set in here--this can be used just to access the camera interface. The general settings are as follows:

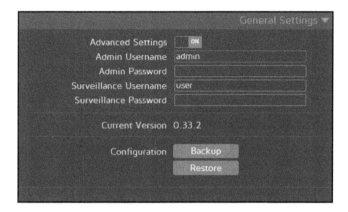

To view all the settings available, you have to set **Advanced Settings** to **ON.** You can see all the settings in the advanced menu, as follows:

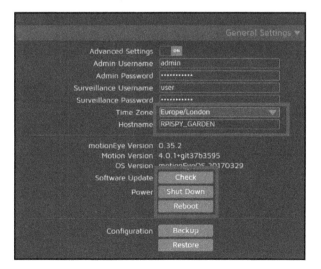

Wireless network

In this section, you can change all the settings relevant to the wireless network. Turn this on if you plan on connecting to the network via a wireless dongle. Raspberry Pi 3 Zero W has an embedded Wi-Fi, so you can probably use it. Thus, there are two things you will need to fill in here:

- **Network name**: Enter the network name or SSID that you would like to connect to
- **Network key**: Enter the network password or network key for the network that you are planning to connect to

You can see the wireless and network menu as follows:

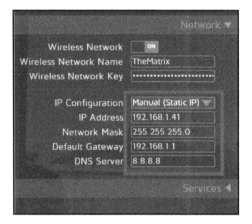

Video device

Under this menu, you will be able to set certain settings with regards to the Raspberry Pi camera device. This means that you can set the camera name and some basic specifications relevant to the environment in which you are planning to set this security system up. So, here is a list of parameters that you can change.

- **Camera Name**: This field is actually just a name for you. Set this to something that represents this camera; for example, if the camera is in the garden, you can name it `Garden Camera`.

- **Camera Device**: This field is the device name of the camera and unfortunately, you cannot edit it.
- **Light Switch Detection:** You can enable this if you want sudden changes; for example, a camera in your room will treat light on/off as motion. To prevent this from happening, use this option.
- **Automatic Brightness:** This will enable software automatic brightness; as a result, this camera will automatically adjust the brightness according to the amount of sun, just as new Android phones adjust their brightness. Note that some cameras already support this feature, so in this case, you don't need to activate this if your camera already handles it.
- **Video Resolution:** Here, you can set the video resolution of the camera. The higher the resolution, the more space you will need on your SD card and the more bandwidth it will need to use in order to stream.
- **Video Rotation:** You can always rotate your video from your Raspberry Pi Zero W board if for any reason, you find upside down stream footage.
- **Frame Rate:** Last but not least, you can set a number of frames that will be sent every second. Again, keep in mind that the higher this is, the smoother the video, but also, this will increase the amount of storage needed and of course the bandwidth.

Now, we will cover the menu settings as they appear in the **Video Device** menu:

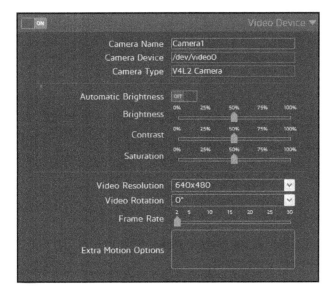

File storage

In this menu, as you can understand, you can specify where you would like the files to be stored on the Raspberry Pi Zero W security camera. You can either set this path on your SD card mounted in the Raspberry Pi board or set this to an external USB connected HDD/SSD drive. Lastly, keep in mind that you can always set this path according to a disk connected to the network. You can see the options available in this menu section as follows:

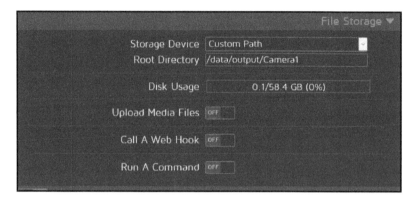

Text Overlay

In here, you can set the text overlay on the output of the camera. If you leave it as it is, the left text reads the camera name and the right text reads the current timestamp. The following screenshot shows the two options that the **Text Overlay** menu provides you with:

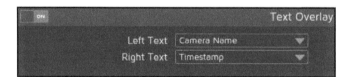

Video Streaming

In this menu, you will be able to set the video streaming options. The options are related to the video that you will see in the browser when you connect to the Raspberry Pi Zero W board. The following is a list of parameters that are necessary and important when you need to lower your video quality or when you have other streaming issues:

- **Streaming Frame Rate**: This is exactly the same as mentioned previously under Video device.
- **Streaming Quality**: Here, you may have to increase or reduce the quality of your video. Again, remember that if you have access to your camera streaming footage over a low bandwidth connection, it is always good practice to reduce the streaming quality. However, if you just need to store the video quality to a hard drive, you may consider maximizing the quality since you do not really need to care about streaming issues.
- **Streaming Image Resizing**: You can enable this feature if you want MotionPie to resize the images before being sent to a browser. But, since we are using the MotionPie software with our Raspberry Pi Zero W board, it is not recommended to do this. So, skip this option and go to the next one.
- **Streaming Port**: It is important to set the streaming port carefully. This is the port that the device will listen to, for connections looking to view the stream. This is the port that you will use from your browser to connect to the camera streaming footage; for example, you can type `http://motionpie:8081` in a browser if your streaming port is `8081`.
- **Motion Optimization**: Lastly, this option will reduce the frame rate whenever no motion is detected. It is useful because you can save a lot of bandwidth. In some cases, we need to reduce as much bandwidth as we can, so keep this option in mind.

The following is an image showing all the options that you can set up and change in the **Video Streaming** menu:

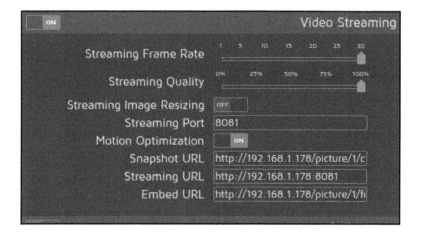

Still images

In this menu, you can set the Raspberry Pi Zero W security camera to take still images whenever motion is triggered, during specific intervals or all the time; for example, you can set this up and capture images every 5 minutes. In some cases, we might need this option.

Motion Detection

This menu is very important. Here, you can activate the Raspberry Pi Zero W security camera motion detection that is included in the software. With this software, you can detect motion in an area and use slack API, as we have seen in the previous chapter, to send notifications back to the user--you can keep log files about what is happening and much more. Make all the adjustments to the settings shown here so that you get better motion detection:

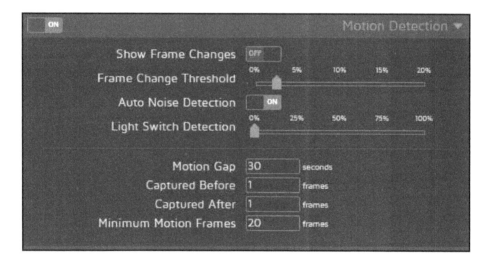

Motion Movies

Here, you can set the Raspberry Pi Zero W board to record movies whenever motion is detected. Since Raspberry Pi Zero W board is small enough to carry and is portable, you a your personal DIY movie recorder.

Motion Notifications

Apart from slack API that provides you notifications, this software allows you to enable and set up email notifications, Webhook notifications, or even run a command whenever motion is detected. This is the most important menu option since this option is the start of home automation. This will allow you to be notified whenever an activity is detected on the camera. The following is the menu as it appears in the MotionPie software menu:

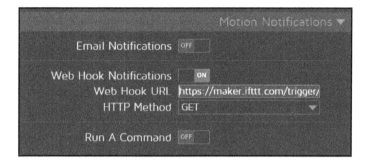

Working Schedule

The last option is the **Working Schedule**. Here, you can set the days and hours of the operation you would like the system to monitor; for example, you may need to leave it off for the weekend. By default, it is 24/7. This option is perfect if you only need it running during specific hours. The following are all the options that you have for this feature on the MotionPie menu:

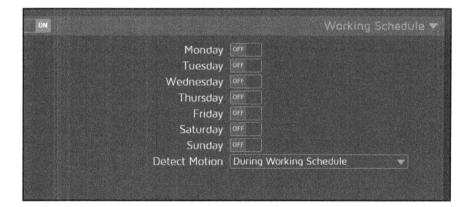

At this point, you should know everything needed to set up your MotionPie software and keep it as simple as you can to maximize its utilization. Next, we will go through the OpenCV installation and see what more we can do.

Installing OpenCV

OpenCV is a library for computer vision. It is well known for face recognition, video tracking, and more image and video processing purposes. At this point, I should say that if you want to use and play with face recognition, this is one of the ultimate libraries that you should use and it is quite hard and difficult to set up. So, in this chapter, we will go through a simple example of how you can run face recognition software on an image. We will not use MotionPie software, so download and install on your SD card your favorite distribution. Assuming that we can power on our Raspberry Pi Zero W board with our loaded distribution, we can start installing the library by referring to the following steps:

1. First of all, SSH your Raspberry Pi Zero W.
2. Change your current directory and navigate to your `home` folder. Then, create a new folder named `opencv_src` and change your current directory again to the folder that you have just created, as follows:

```
cd ~
mkdir opencv_src
cd opencv_src
```

3. Now, we have to get the appropriate code from GitHub. We can do this by cloning the appropriate repository with the following command:

```
git clone https://github.com/Itseez/opencv.git
```

4. Then, change your current directory to the one you just cloned with the following command:

```
cd opencv/
```

5. Create a new directory named `release` and change the current directory to it with the following command:

```
mkdir release
cd release/
```

6. Now, we have to make and build the library that we have downloaded. This may take some time, so be patient. We can do this with the following command:

```
cmake -D CMAKE_BUILD_TYPE=RELEASE -D CMAKE_INSTALL_PREFIX=/usr/local ..
```

7. Now execute the `make` command, as follows:

```
make
```

8. Lastly, install the library we have downloaded with the following command:

```
sudo make install
```

 More information can be found on the official website of OpenCV here: http://docs.opencv.org/2.4/doc/tutorials/introduction/linux_install/linux_install.html

Face recognition

Assuming that you have successfully installed OpenCV, we can test this out by simply importing cv with Python. Open up a Terminal and type `python` to start the shell and then, type the following command:

```
import cv2
```

If everything goes OK and there are no errors on the screen, you should be fine. Else, go back and reinstall OpenCV as described previously. Now, let's break down the actual code, which you can find and download from the following link:

```
https://github.com/shantnu/FaceDetect/
```

In the `face_detect.py` script, the `abba.png` image, and the `haarcascade_frontalface_default.xml` are the following. When executing the file, you have to pass these two arguments:

```
# Get user supplied values
imagePath = sys.argv[1]
cascPath = sys.argv[2]
```

As a result, you first pass in the image and then, cascade names. In the following example, we will use the Abba image as the source input image and the default cascade for detecting almost all the faces provided by OpenCV. With the following code, we will create the cascade and initialize it with our default face cascade:

```
# Create the haar cascade
faceCascade = cv2.CascadeClassifier(cascPath)
```

With this command, we simply load into the memory the face cascade so that it is ready for use later on. At this point, it is important to remember that the cascade is just an XML file that contains data to detect faces and nothing more. If you have knowledge about image processing, you can go and modify the file or create a new one:

```
# Read the image
image = cv2.imread(imagePath)
gray = cv2.cvtColor(image, cv2.COLOR_BGR2GRAY)
```

With the `imread` command, we can simply read the image given and then, we convert it to grayscale. This is important because many operations in OpenCV are done in grayscale and not in RGB images. The following function detects the face and is the actual key part of the software. We have the following options that we can adjust here:

- First of all, the `detectMultiScale` function is a general function that detects objects. Depending on the cascade that we provide as input, it will detect the object that the cascade describes:
  - The first option here is the grayscale image.
  - The second is the `scaleFactor`, and this is important since some faces according to the are deeper in the image and other are closer. It is important to adjust the `scaleFactor` so that the software knows how big the face is which it is looking for.
  - Next, it is important to know that the detection algorithm uses a moving window to detect objects:
    - The `minNeighbors` defines how many objects are detected near the current one before it outputs and declares that the face was found.

- Also, the `minSize` is actually the size of each window used. You can experiment with different values and choose what works best for you. Thus, the function returns a list of rectangles, as you can see in the following image, where it believes that it has found a face. There may be some false positives but we can fix them with the `scaleFactor` option. Next, we will loop over where it thinks it found something.

```
print "Found {0} faces!".format(len(faces))

    # Draw a rectangle around the faces
    for (x, y, w, h) in faces:
        cv2.rectangle(image, (x, y), (x+w, y+h), (0, 255, 0), 2)
```

As a result, we have four values returned. The *X* and *Y* are the location of the rectangle, and *W* and *H* are the rectangle's width and height. We can use these four values to simply create a rectangle using the building function of the library. So, we do this with the following command:

```
cv2.imshow("Faces found" ,image)
cv2.waitKey(0)
```

Lastly, we display the final image after the rectangles are inserted. To test this out, run the following command:

```
python face_detect.py abba.png haarcascade_frontalface_default.xml
```

There may arise a possible issue with this command. If it is not working, you may need to open the `face_detect.py` file and replace the line, as follows:

```
Flags = cv2.cv.CV_HAAR_SCALE_IMAGE
Flags = cv2.CASCADE_SCALE_IMAGE
```

The result will be the following image with green rectangles added:

Source: https://github.com/shantnu/FaceDetect/

You can test this with your own images and see what the software finds out. The quality of the image is crucial for this function to work properly. Also, the right scaleFactor has to be modified according to the size of the faces in the image. You should always keep in mind that the results will never be 100% accurate. However, you will get good enough results in most cases! If we test this out with another image, as follows, you can see that it detects faces that do not exist:

Source: `https://github.com/shantnu/FaceDetect/`

If you change the `scaleFactor` to 1.2, you get the right response from the software as you can see in the following image; it detects the faces:

Source: `https://github.com/shantnu/FaceDetect/`

Summary

In this chapter, we went through the installation of the MotionPie software, which is easy to install and use. You should be able to connect your camera and add your Raspberry Pi camera to your projects. Next, we will go step by step about how you can create your own portable speakers with the new lightweight Pi board.

7
Portable Speakers

In the previous chapter, we went through developing a security camera in a step-by-step manner and connecting multiple cameras with our Raspberry Pi Zero W board. In this chapter, we will create something different. Raspberry Pi Zero W is not only useful for security projects but also for other DIY solutions. So, here we will see how to create your personal portable speakers. After completing this project, you will be able to connect your portable speakers and hear your own music or expand already existing projects that you must have developed. Lastly, we will add another feature, which will let you play music depending on your mood. Hence, in this chapter, we will go through the following sections:

- Market speakers
- Software setup
- Networking
- Music on Pi
- Speaker setup
- Mood selection

Market speakers

If you search the market, you will find many different modules available to buy. Raspberry Pi calls these modules extensions and, depending on your project, you can buy the appropriate extension to increase your Raspberry Pi capabilities and make your project easier since there are many things already implemented. This means that you do not have to code and develop everything from scratch. Sometimes, it is worth spending time and searching for modules and similar projects. Speakers are one of them and you can buy them directly for your Raspberry Pi.

Unfortunately, Raspberry Pi Zero W has no audio input/output. So, there are two ways to play music, which are as follows:

- From HDMI
- From Bluetooth or Wi-Fi

There are some tutorials on how you can play audio from the HDMI port, but in this section we will go through playing audio via bluetooth or Wi-Fi. One popular market speakers is the mini portable speakers for Raspberry Pi that you can find directly from the Pi Hut shop. They are low cost speakers and work great with Raspberry Pi boards. The following is an image of what they look like:

It is working on 5V and can play audio for about seven hours. So, with something like this, we can create your portable speaker.

 More information about this speaker can be found at `https://thepihut.com/products/mini-portable-speaker-for-the-raspberry-pi?variant=897680793`.

Of course have in mind that they need battery, so either have a powerbank with you or buy some other battery stuff. This is really up to you.

Software setup

Before we start connecting all the things together in our Raspberry Pi Zero W board, we have to burn a new SD card with the appropriate image. So, download the Pi Music Box zip from the official website in the following link: `http://www.pimusicbox.com/`. Now, you need to install this software in your SD card so use *dd* tool or anything else that you are familiar with depending on your operating system and perform the following steps:

1. Insert the SD card in your Raspberry Pi Zero W board. In case you are using an external Wi-Fi Dongle (for any reason), you might consider to edit the `config settings.ini` file. The location of the file is in the SD card that you just wrote. Assuming that your board is equipped with Wi-Fi and bluetooth, you will skip the previous step, but for anyone out there that prefers the hard way or has Raspberry Pi Zero board (which is quite similar), he will have to edit the username and password of the Wi-Fi settings.
2. Next, you need to provide internet access to your Raspberry Pi Zero W.
3. We need to find the IP address of the Raspberry Pi Zero W board. After that, we have to ssh to that IP address at port `22` and you will be prompted to insert username and password. Type the default username and password since you haven't changed them and you should be in the Pi by now.
4. Assuming that it is all set, try and open up a browser and go to the following address: `http://musicbox.local`.

If for any reason you have troubles with the preceding steps, you will need to use the IP of the Raspberry Pi. Remember that you learned how to get and find this IP in the previous chapters. If you have your Pi connected to a screen, you can find the IP from the command line by typing the following command:

```
ifconfig
```

Once connected in your browser, you should be presented with a screen like the one shown in the following screenshot:

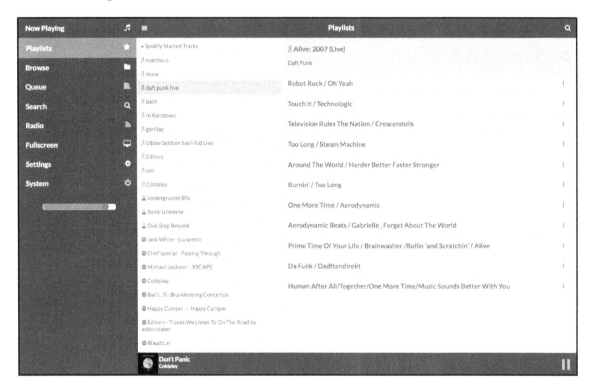

Now, it is important to understand that we will be streaming this over the local network and not the internet. Streaming or connecting devices over the internet requires more actions to set this up. We will not go through all this stuff in this chapter. Remember to update and upgrade your system when installing the latest Raspberry Pi distribution. You can update your system by typing the following command:

```
sudo apt-get update
```

You can upgrade with all the latest packages using the following command:

```
sudo apt-get upgrade
```

At this point, you should have the latest system that can connect to your speaker and play your favorite music.

Networking

In this section, we will go through some settings that we can change to make it work and set this up in our local network. After that, the MusicBox player should be operating in your network and everything should be connected. Let's look at the following settings:

- **Network name**: This name is actually the SSID or the name of your Wi-Fi network. It can be changed from your router interface by visiting the URL `http://192.168.1.1` in most of the cases. If not, check your manual for the appropriate URL of your router.
- **Wi-Fi password**: Obviously, this is the field where you have to place the Wi-Fi password of your network. Once more, the password can be changed by visiting the link that we visited earlier. For many reasons, it is important to always add a strong password that includes letters, capital letters, symbols, and numbers randomly.
- **Workgroup**: This field is the workgroup name of your local Windows network. When connecting your Windows machine to a network, you are prompted to choose the group in which you will belong.
- **SSD**: As we already know, ssh is always useful for many reasons so it is advised to turn this on for later modifications. On the other hand, if you want to just complete the projects and do not change anything in the Raspberry Pi Zero W board, you can always leave it as it is.

MusicBox

In this section, we will go through some settings and mention some tips for your MusicBox. You may not need to change many things, but it is always good to know what choices we have:

- **Device name**: This is the name of your Raspberry Pi Zero W board in your local network. The default name is MusicBox, so if for any reason you want to change it, go ahead. Notice that the URL that we were using had the name MusicBox, so if you change this, you will need to visit a different URL according to the name.
- **Autoplay URL**: Here you can insert a URL so that the Raspberry Pi Zero W board can start playing a radio station or stream when the device boots up. Consider that you might have to increase the waiting time a bit so that the boot-up process is complete before the initiation of the MusicBox.

- **Wait time**: Here is the time that the MusicBox waits before starting to play the URL. As we mentioned earlier, it is wise to increase this a bit. Remember that the numbers are in seconds. A 20-second delay would be a good choice.
- **Root password**: The default root password is MusicBox, but you should consider changing this to something more secure. It is almost necessary to do this, especially if you are going to enable SSH access.
- **AirPlay streaming**: Here we can stream directly from the mobile phone to the Raspberry Pi Music Server. If you enable this option, it should show up the Airplay device list.
- **DLNA/uPnP/OpenHome streaming**: Since we may need to stream the MusicBox over some protocols, we can enable the appropriate one from this section.

Audio

As far as the audio is concerned, there are a few options here. The initial volume is the default volume of the device when it starts. Next, the audio output is the output of the audio. Here, you can manually select the output for the audio. Lastly, the down sample USB can be enabled if you have any kind of trouble with the quality of the audio when playing. Usually, older boards may need to turn this on. The latest ones are just fine and do not need this option.

Music files

Here, we will see the option of music files that we can play and how we can connect a playlist with the software:

1. Firstly, the **Scan Music Files** can be enabled to scan any files when booting, but this will slow down the procedure.
2. Next, the **Network Drive**, which may be the best option here, requires, of course, to have a network drive setup that has all your music, but you can connect it easily with the MusicBox and play music directly from it. One thing that usually goes wrong is the setup of the username and password used. So, have a second look at that in case of any issues.
3. Lastly, the **Resize Filesystem** option is quite important since when automatically rebooting, it gives us access to the entire SD card.

Online music services

Now let's just move on to another subject about the online music services such as Spotify or YouTube. There are hundreds of services out there such as Spotify, YouTube, or even SoundCloud that can be connected with the MusicBox and each one of them is pretty much straightforward. We will not go through it in this chapter, but, as always, if you want to expand your playlist and have one of the services mentioned earlier connected to your Raspberry Pi zero W, you can Google for more information.

Security

Keep in mind that the MusicBox may be a good option, but it is not secure enough to run outside a firewall. So, keep your local firewall up and always protect yourself with a strong password. Lastly, there is one more option that we may consider to access. So, if you want to access the mopify GUI instead of the Pi MusicBox GUI, simply go to your browser and type:

```
musicbox.local/mopify
```

Again, replace the `musicbox.local` with the IP of the Raspberry Pi. Mopify is a GUI designed for spotify only, so if you want to use the other services, then you will need to use the Pi music box GUI.

I hope you now have a fully working Raspberry Pi music player up and running.

Sound players

Since there are many times that we are connected to our Raspberry Pi Zero W board via ssh, it is important to know how to control the volume and any possible audio from the terminal. When no Graphical User Interface or GUI is presented, we do not have so many options to control the sound volume. A good idea is to use a command called alsamixer, which allows us to easily change and have full control of the input/output sounds in our Raspberry Pi Zero W board or our Linux device. Usually, it is preinstalled in your system, but if it is not, you can always find it using the following command:

```
aptitude search alsa
```

That way it will list your packages that you can install similar to `alsa`. The `aptitude` command is a useful command to find similar packages. Here is the result, searching for `alsa`:

```
mark@zeus ~ $ aptitude search alsa
v   alsa                         -
v   alsa:i386                    -
i   alsa-base                    - ALSA driver configuration files
v   alsa-base:i386               -
p   alsa-firmware-loaders        - ALSA software loaders for specific hardwar
p   alsa-firmware-loaders:i386   - ALSA software loaders for specific hardwar
p   alsa-oss                     - ALSA wrapper for OSS applications
p   alsa-oss:i386                - ALSA wrapper for OSS applications
p   alsa-source                  - ALSA driver sources
p   alsa-tools                   - Console based ALSA utilities for specific
p   alsa-tools:i386              - Console based ALSA utilities for specific
p   alsa-tools-gui               - GUI based ALSA utilities for specific hard
p   alsa-tools-gui:i386          - GUI based ALSA utilities for specific hard
i   alsa-utils                   - Utilities for configuring and using ALSA
p   alsa-utils:i386              - Utilities for configuring and using ALSA
p   alsamixergui                 - graphical soundcard mixer for ALSA soundca
p   alsamixergui:i386            - graphical soundcard mixer for ALSA soundca
v   alsaplayer                   -
v   alsaplayer:i386              -
p   alsaplayer-alsa              - alsaplayer output module for ALSA
p   alsaplayer-alsa:i386         - alsaplayer output module for ALSA
p   alsaplayer-common            - audio player (common files)
```

Now, let's use alsamixer to control the volume of your computer. You can type the following in your terminal to start the alsamixer:

Alsamixer

You will now see something like the following depending on the devices that are connected in your Linux system.

You can exit the alsamixer by pressing the *Q* key. Now, you have another tool in your hands when playing with sound to control it through the terminal and without any monitor with graphical user interface:

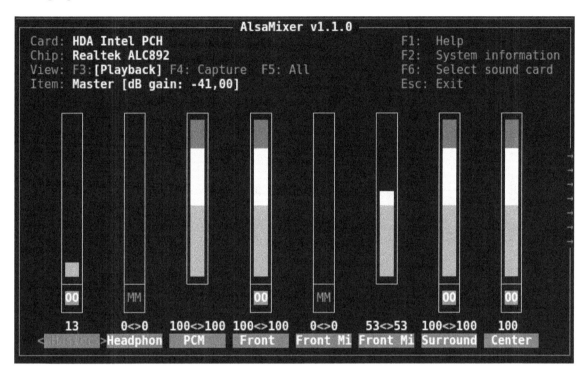

Connect your speaker

At this point, we should be ready to connect your speakers with the Raspberry Pi Zero W board. The easiest way to do that is by going to the **Program** menu and then **Preferences** and clicking on the **Bluetooth Manager**. Your bluetooth speakers should always search to sync with a device. Assuming that your speaker is waiting to sync, click on search and you should be taken to an interface. Now, you should be able to pair the two devices. If any problems occur, you should click on **Connect again** and wait to be connected. After that, you should be okay and you can test this out by playing a YouTube song. Go ahead.

Music on Pi

Our Raspberry Pi Zero W board is a Linux computer that allows us to do almost whatever we want as we had a Linux desktop computer in front of us. So, to upload music to our Raspberry Pi Zero W, we can use the old fashion way of using USB devices and transfer a huge amount of songs and playlists. On the other hand, we can use the following command to directly download songs from YouTube:

```
Youtube-dl <youtube-link>
```

If you see any error messages, it is probably because you do not have `youtube-dl` installed. You can do this easily by typing the following command:

```
sudo apt-get install youtube-dl
```

Now, you should be fine and ready to download music from your YouTube account directly to your Raspberry Pi Zero W. `youtube-dl` software have many options and you might want to view details about it using the manual page. To open and read any manual page in a Linux system type the following command:

```
man <command>
```

In our case, the `<command>` is `youtube-dl`.

On the other hand, if with any way you transfer your music on your Raspberry Pi Zero W, you can play the music with some players such as `vlc` or Audacious. VLC is a well-known video player, but it has something that you might now know. It can be started from the terminal and play without a graphical user interface. When all we have is a terminal, sometimes it is useful to go and read the manual page and find whether a common program can be used otherwise. To start `vlc` from the terminal, you can type the following command:

```
vlc <options>
```

Here, the options can be relevant to the song that you want to play, the video, or even the playlist. For example, to start the `vlc` with GUI and play a song type the following command:

```
vlc <song name>
```

The result of the preceding command is as follows:

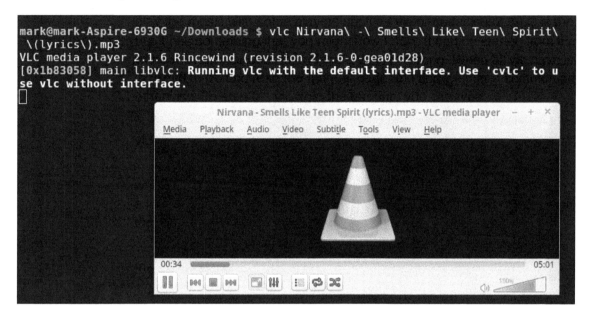

```
mark@mark-Aspire-6930G ~/Downloads $ vlc Nirvana\ -\ Smells\ Like\ Teen\ Spirit\
 \(lyrics\).mp3
VLC media player 2.1.6 Rincewind (revision 2.1.6-0-gea01d28)
[0x1b83058] main libvlc: Running vlc with the default interface. Use 'cvlc' to u
se vlc without interface.
```

However, if you want to start `vlc` by only using the terminal and without opening any GUI, you can type the following command:

```
cvlc <song>
```

The result of the preceding command is as follows:

```
mark@mark-Aspire-6930G ~/Downloads $ cvlc Nirvana\ -\ Smells\ Like\ Teen\ Spirit\ \(lyrics\).mp3
VLC media player 2.1.6 Rincewind (revision 2.1.6-0-gea01d28)
[0x16993c8] dummy interface: using the dummy interface module...
```

 For more information visit the official page at `https://wiki.videolan.org/Command_line/` and in the manual page of VLC by typing the following command:

```
man vlc
```

Lastly, Audacious is another cool music player with graphical user interface or GUI and is capable to change various themes. The following screenshot shows what the default theme will look like:

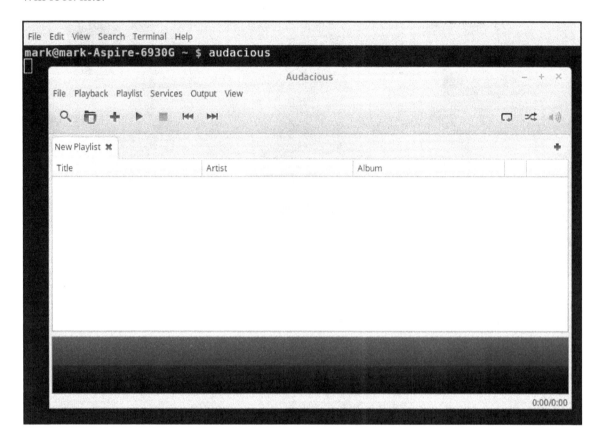

Mood selection

By now, you should have a complete system that plays music and is connected to your Raspberry Pi Zero W board. Now, to make it more smart, let's add a mood selection system that plays the appropriate music playlist according to your mood. To do that, we first need to create a few playlists that will correspond to our mood. For example, let's define the first playlist as **Acoustic Playlist** and the second one as **Rock Playlist**. We can do that in many ways, one of which is to create two folders with the appropriate names and place some songs in each of them. Using cvlc that we mentioned earlier, we will be able to connect our music player with any script. So what is left is the trigger system.

The trigger system will be implemented according to the equipment that you have. The most easy mood selection system that we can create will consist of two buttons each one of them will trigger the corresponding playlist. So, first we need to connect two buttons in our Raspberry Pi Zero W board, and then, write some Python code to determine which button was pressed and which playlist will be the one that starts playing.

Hardware

As far as the hardware is concerned, and according to the Raspberry Pi zero W pinout, we need to connect each button to the pin. The two buttons must be connected to the pins 17 and 27 according to the following schematic:

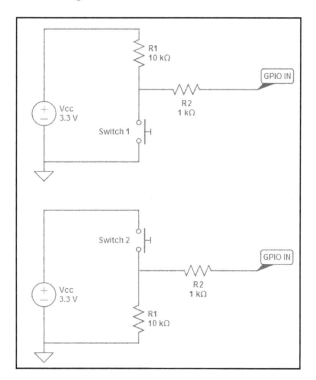

Code

The following code is a Python script and be executed after saving it as `script.py` by typing the following command in your Python console:

```
python script.py
```

Now, let's go through the following lines and see what we have developed. Firstly, we need to import the time library so that we can pause the `while` loop later on:

```
import time
```

Next, we need to initialize a previous input variable to `0`. Here, we assume that the button was not pressed. We also create a new variable named `state`, which indicates the state of the button. `0` means that the button is released and `1` indicated that it is pressed:

```
prev_input = 0
state = 0
```

Next, we create a `while` loop and we read the two input GPIO pins:

```
while True:
    input = GPIO.input(17)
    input = GPIO.input(27)
```

After that, we need to check the input state and if the button was pressed, then we need to check whether the state is pressed or released. If it was pressed, we change it to released and if it was released we change it to pressed:

```
if ((not prev_input) and input):
    print("Button pressed")
    if(state == 0):
        state = 1
        // code to play the first playlist
    else:
        state = 0
        // code to play the second playlist
#update previous input
prev_input = input
#slight pause to debounce
time.sleep(0.05)
```

Now, the code that we need to add to the preceding block of code is one or two lines so that we can play the playlist. For example, we can add the following code:

```
vlc song1.mp3
```

Next we can add state1:

```
vlc song2.mp3
```

Then we can add state2.

Summary

In this chapter, we saw how we can create some portable speakers, so that we are able to play our favorite music everywhere. Since music changes the mood, an interactive way of understanding the reader's mood and playing specific playlists was added in the last sections. Furthermore, we saw how you can control the volume and the audio of your Linux system through the terminal. Lastly, we mentioned some music and video players necessary for your everyday audio or video interaction with the Raspberry Pi Zero W.

In the next chapter, we will go through developing a small hosting service in our home using only the Pi wireless board.

8
WebPi Hosting

In the previous chapter, you learned how to create some portable speakers with your Raspberry Pi Zero W board. In this chapter, you will go through the most important topic when developing a website and hosting all the files in your Raspberry Pi Zero W. You will gain a general idea of client-server communication regarding web hosting services, some basic knowledge of web development and the way in which you should access and transfer your files from your local computer to the Raspberry Pi Zero W. Lastly, this chapter will conclude with some security tips and issues that you may face when hosting your files at home. To sum up, in this chapter, we will cover the following topics:

- Client-server communication
- Web hosting
- Web design and development
- Networking administration

Web hosting

In this section, we will define what web hosting is and what one must do to get his own personal web hosting service up. You should see this as an introduction to the rest of the chapter; so as always, the first step is to define exactly what we are doing here and what we should do in case we have no Raspberry Pi Zero W at our hands. There are several hosting services providing different solutions depending on needs of the customer. In the rest of the section, we will also describe the possible options that a customer has and the advantages or drawbacks of some of them.

Definition

Web hosting is a means by which you can host your files or website on a computer, where you or everyone has access to it from all over the world; for example, an e-shop has a website hosted on a server, and you are able to access and interact with the server through your browser or your mobile phone. Thus, the web hosting is more about the server side, how you can save your files and serve them to anyone that requests them. To make this easier to understand, let's look the following image, where the client (computer) is requesting a website using his browser, and the server is responding back with the website:

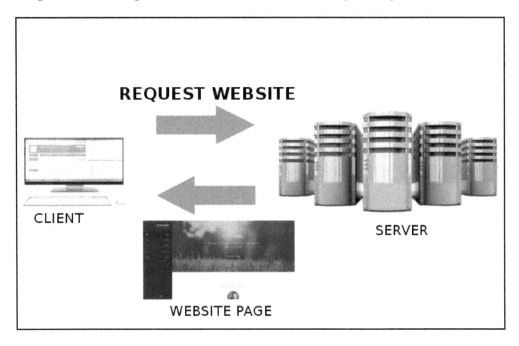

As we can see in the preceding image, the client is requesting a website from the server and the server serves that webpage to the client; thus, we have two communication directions and two arrows. The user may be using a desktop PC or mobile phone; he may also be using Firefox, Google Chrome, or any other browser. The server is usually a big server building similar to the preceding image but can also be a small pocket-size Raspberry Pi Zero W board. The important thing is that we always have a client who requests things and a server ready to respond if of course the client is authorized to receive these files. In this chapter, the client will be us or anyone in the world, and the server will be our Raspberry Pi Zero W board. Now, let's see some options we normally have when we buy a hosting package.

Hosting services

Usually, the big hosting services have more than one solution. This is because we all have different needs. People have different needs; thus, almost everyone has different packages; for example, you may have a few MB of the total space, or have unlimited space and one database, or more features such as one click WordPress installation, and more. Depending on your needs, you obviously choose a service with the lowest cost for your company or your personal need. Next, you can see an image from Top Host displaying the hosting services they provide:

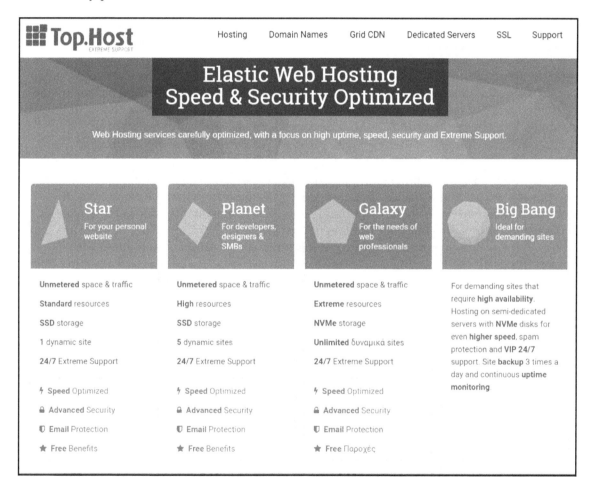

As you can see, there are four options: in the first, you have one dynamic site; in the second, five dynamic sites; in the third, unlimited; and in the last, you have everything. Obviously, not every hosting company provides all the services from the image but they all have the same logic. Generally speaking, if you want to host some files or a website of a total size < 500 MB, you should be fine and the cost is not too much. However, if you want to host a website for a company such as an e-shop or similar, you need to invest in a good server such as the preceding one. It should be clear that when you have a company, you do not host your e-shop on a Raspberry Pi Zero W board. It may work but you have zero user reliability or support.

Domain name

Another thing to consider before completing your purchase is the selection of your domain name. As we will discuss in later sections, apart from web hosting, we need a domain name so that people can remember our website. Servers and, as a result, websites have an IP Address. This means that the `facebook.com` website has an IP address, such as `157.240.9.35`. Imagine if there was no `facebook.com` and all users had to type `157.240.9.35` every single time they wanted to use the website. There is no way that the internet could have such dimensions as it has today using this kind of interaction with servers and requesting websites. To conclude, this is the reason that we came up with domain names; each website has a domain name that obviously is easier to remember since it consists of letters. Picking your domain name may be straightforward, but there are some things that you should consider before paying for it. As we said, a domain name is something similar to `facebook.com`, `linkedin.com`, `vasilistzivaras.gr`, or anything that makes your website unique in the world. There is no domain name that corresponds to two websites. First of all, it is important to know that a domain name is quite important for **Search Engine Optimization** (**SEO**). SEO means that the name of the website is a variable in the Google search algorithm. If we do not want to make it available to the internet and we need the website for personal use, that is OK and you probably do not have to buy a domain name, as I think that you can remember an IP address. However, if you are creating a website to be made available to the entire internet and adding it to Google's search engine result list, then the URL or the domain name should be something that really represents your website; for example, it is stupid to have a website about clothes with the domain name `catsanddogs.com`. At this point, I should say that many hosting providers give you free hosting for a small website when buying a domain name. This is how I, personally, have developed my website `vasilistzivaras.gr`.

DNS

Furthermore, it is important to introduce another term relevant to web hosting and domain names. We do not have to buy anything here, but it is crucial to know what a DNS does. We talked about web hosting, so there is a computer that hosts our files. We also talked about the domain name, so there is a URL or a name that corresponds to our server's IP address. When a client types our domain name in a web browser, the computer needs to know the IP address. So, a **Domain Name Server** (**DNS**) is a system that matches IP addresses with domain names. This is not something that we have to buy, but is something that we or our website administration needs to set up.

Setup

Now, let's see what happens after we buy a hosting service. At this point, you should have an IP address for your website, username, and password. You should go to the link that is contained in your verification email and after the login, you are prompted to pdesk or some other interface on which you can set up your hosting and domain names. I will define a list with the actions we need to perform and later on, in further sections, we will discuss solutions for this kind of action-issue. So, after buying a website, you need to:

- Transfer your files or website to the hosting server
- Set up DNS according to your domain name

If you are familiar with web development, you must have already come up with some questions. There are some issues born here; for example, how will we transfer the files to the hosting service? Usually, drag and drop works but not always, especially in our Raspberry Pi Zero W board but we will discuss this subject later. Next, how do we match the domain name with the server IP address? Furthermore, what if I want to make a minor change? Do I have to upload all the files again? As you can see, web hosting requires some experience and is not straightforward for many users out there. This is why many hosting services have a live support 24/7 and a ticket troubleshooting page.

Client-server communication

Now that you know what web hosting is, you should have questions. Since you are always the client and you have a server at your home or somewhere in the world, how do you communicate with it? How can any client communicate with the server and get his response? The client-server communication idea will be described in this section and by the end of the section, the definition of web hosting and the way it works should be crystal clear.

Client request

As we have seen in the previous section, the client's job is to request things. He requests a website's files or anything served from a server. The connection of a client to a server is shown in the next figure, where the client makes a request through an application:

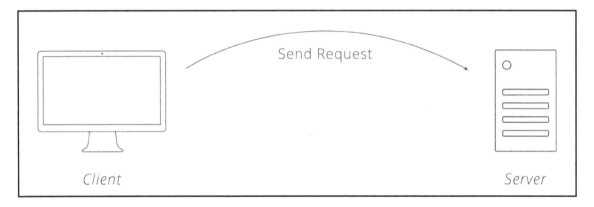

Note that a client is usually a person, but without doubt, a client can be another server. Client-server communication is a basic idea, where the client requests over HTTP or HTTPS protocol files from a server. If the server does not have those files then, the server itself can request them from another server or respond with Error 404: File not found.

Communication protocols

There are many protocols according to which a request can be completed. HTTP and FTP are such protocols and we will look at them in this section:

- **HTTP (Hyper Text Transfer Protocol)**: HTTP is the primary technology protocol on the Web that allows linking and browsing. On the other hand, **HTTPS** stands for **Hyper Text Transfer Protocol Secure**. Some websites use HTTPS, such as facebook.com, and others that use HTTP usually have an administrator that has no idea what S in HTTPS stands for or for some kind of reason did not update the hosting service with SSL. If you go through the purchase of a hosting package, you will probably be prompted to buy and add SSL to your website. SSL means that the HTTP will be equipped with the S at the end so that your website is more secure.

- **FTP (File Transfer Protocol)**: FTP, on the other hand, is usually used when we want to transfer files; for example, there are many FTP servers, such as `http://ftp.ntua.gr`, where they do not serve a website, only files. When you are connecting to a server via a specific protocol, you have to use a specific port number. Communication protocols operate at specific ports. HTTP(S) uses port `80` and FPT uses port `21`. When you set up a server at your home, you have to specify the port that it will be running on and if, for example, you are running your server on port `2356`, then you have to visit the `<http(s)/ftp>://<server-IP/domain-name>:<port>` URL. First, you define the protocol that you are using, then the IP address or the domain, and lastly the port. To sum up, your request should follow the simple rule `<Protocol, IP, Port>`. As a result, we can have many different client requests, as follows:

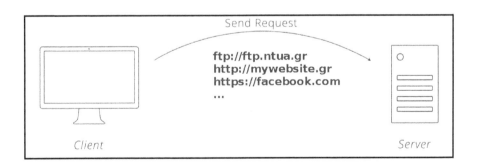

In the next section, we will talk about request handling performed by the server side.

Server response

In the previous section, we discussed how a client can make different requests. All of them end up somewhere and someone must handle them. Either, respond with the appropriate files and response or with some error message. Next, you can see that as soon as the server received a request from the server, it responded as follows:

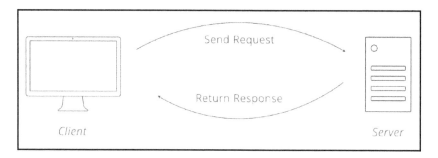

Now, we will talk about this response and what happens before the response reaches the client side. Let's say that someone talks to you and asks something. The natural thing that you always do is process this request and then respond. This is exactly what a server does. The server receives hundreds of requests from all over the world and processes these requests using appropriate methods to find out exactly what each one of them wants. Imagine that a request is like a magic box, inside which we have a protocol, the names of all the files requested optionally, a username, and a password. The server opens this box and distinguishes all these components. Depending on the protocol name, it sends the rest of the components on the appropriate handlers, which depending on some other parameters send data to other handlers, and so on. There is a whole procedure over there in which your request is being analyzed and your response is being prepared. In the following figure, you can see a simple demonstration of what is going on on the server side:

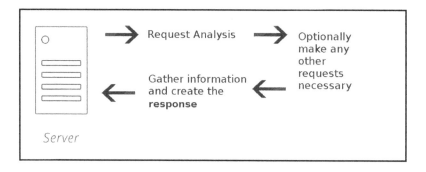

As soon as the server has all the information needed, it sends the response to the IP address found in the request message.

Proxy servers and caching

Another important part are the proxy servers, where they actually act as an intermediate server between the client and the actual server. They are usually used for security purposes and anonymity. As soon as the client creates a request, the request reaches the proxy server, and the proxy server is then in charge of determining what to do. This way, the client does not *see* the actual server and cannot attack him directly or cause any other bad things. Furthermore, servers usually use cache memory. Caching is something that YouTube uses, big companies use, and if you want fast responses, it is crucial. The basic idea behind caching is that a chasing server has the files that you request and can respond back to you very fast. They are usually not so big and cannot store everything. Imagine them as another server that stands in front of the actual big one, where only the top 100 requests are stored. It is like a shield, where you first hit the cache server and then, the actual server. If you search or request something that is already requested by many users, you will probably find it there and get a fast response. If the proxy server does not have the file, it creates a request from the web server and responds but in this case, you will have to wait a bit longer. In the following figure, we can see that the client requests something from the server but he actually communicates with the proxy server. The proxy server is in front of the main server and acts like a firewall or another security layer.

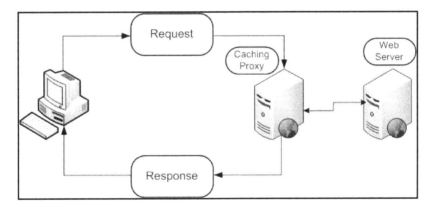

Website development

Going further, this project is about hosting your personal or any kind of website on Raspberry Pi Zero W. In this section, we will not have an analytic discussion on how you can develop your website. However, I will mention different ways that you can work and give a general direction on what you should and should not do. Some websites have a total size in MBs and others may go up to GBs depending on the size of files that are necessary. Thus, choosing wisely when selecting the type of website that you will host is quite important and if you skip this, you may encounter problems, errors, and many more issues.

The development of a website depends one hundred percent on your need. You can create a simple website with buttons for your IoT project so that you can have access to your other Arduino or Raspberry Pi devices; or you can create a temporary simple responsive website using HTML, CSS, and JavaScript; or you can even set up a database and create an e-shop. Obviously, this section will not tell you how to create an advanced website, but it will guide you through some basic steps on how you can develop the simplest one. Let's say that the scenario here is to develop a website on which you click on a button and open a door. The website should have a button and a text that indicates the button's activity. On your local machine, open up your favorite editor and create a simple HTML file, where you have inserted a button. The code is as follows:

```
<!DOCTYPE html>
<html>
<body>
This button activate something:<button type="button" onclick="alert('Hello
world!')">Active</button>
</body>
</html>
```

First, we define the DOCTYPE as HTML. Next, inside the `body` tag, we need to create a button that when clicked on, says `Hello world`. Obviously, you have to change this and link it with the Arduino project that you might have. The preceding website looks similar to the following image:

This button activate something: Active

After clicking on the **Active** button, you will see a pop-up window as follows:

XAMPP/LAMPP

XAMPP package is a free package to download and is actually a set of tools necessary for running your website. XAMPP has Apache server, MySQL, and some other functionalities. You can download XAMPP from `https://www.apachefriends.org/index.html`.

XAMPP allows you to install this software and control whether you want to activate and start the Apache server necessary to run and execute PHP code and MySQL, necessary if your website has an interaction with databases, such as WordPress. The XAMPP control panel looks as follows:

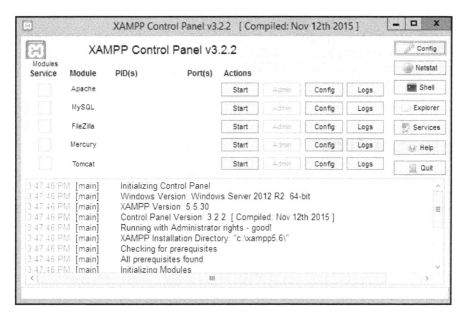

Through this control panel, you can start the Apache server, MySQL service, and many other services. For the sake of simplicity, we will start only the Apache server and the MySQL service. Note that in the case of any errors, close the applications that are running on port `80` or `8080`, such as Skype or Steam. If everything goes OK, Apache and MySQL will be marked with a green color.

XAMPP creates a local server. As a result, the machine that XAMPP is installed on is the actual server. You need to install XAMPP on the Raspberry Pi Zero W board. On the official website, you will find that XAMPP is available for many operating systems. XAMPP has a specific location where you need to place files, so the whole thing will work. In Windows, the location is under `C:\xampp\htdocs\`, and in Linux, it is under the path `/opt/lampp/htdoc`. Obviously, since Raspberry Pi is Linux, you will need to create a folder inside the htdocs folder after installation.

Accessing the website

To access your website locally, you only need the IP of the Raspberry Pi board. With this IP, any device, computer, or mobile phone in your local network can visit the URL `<ipdevice>/<folder>`, where `<ipdevice>` is the IP address of your Raspberry Pi Zero W board, and `<folder>` is the name of the folder you have just created in the `htdocs` folder. If you do all the steps described previously, you will see nothing because we have no web page. Now, inside the folder, we need to create an `index.html` or `index.php` file containing our website. The Apache server will always search for the name index first. If there is no file with the name index, it will list all the possible files that you have in that folder. In the following section, you will learn how to transfer and upload a website to this folder.

Remote control

Determined by the location where you are hosting your website or your files, there are different ways to access and modify your files. Usually, web development is not a one-time job, and this means that we do not upload the files, exit the server, and the job is done. You may need to come back, make changes, upload new files, and many other things. It is always important to have simple and easy ways to do these types of tasks, with and without graphical user interface. There are two main protocols used to control and interact with a remote server. The first one is via **SSH**, as we have already seen, and the second one is using **SFTP**.

SSH

SSH, which stands for Secure Shell, is an old but still a good way to connect to your remote server, usually at port `22`. The ssh is the advanced telnet communication that many people use to connect to their server. To use SSH, you have to install an SSH server on the server side and use an SSH client on the client side. Since the server port `22` will be up and running waiting for incoming connections, you can easily open up your SSH client and log in to the server with your credentials. Next, we will mention some ways of doing this using Windows and Linux. After that, we will analyze a script that does it automatically. It will save time and make this connection more secure.

SSH clients

Depending on your operating system, you have to download and use an appropriate SSH client. All SSH clients and programs need to know the IP address to which you will be connecting and the port number. This procedure will be mentioned step by step and after this, we will make it automatic. So, let's see what choices we have for different operating systems.

Windows

For Windows, users use a common ssh client called PuTTY that works well and is free. From Windows 10 and later, there will probably be command tools that allow you to open ssh connections. However, since Windows users are familiar with GUI, let's stay in the program mentioned previously. PuTTY can be downloaded from the official website for free:

```
https://www.chiark.greenend.org.uk/~sgtatham/putty/latest.html
```

On their website, there are many links to different versions, but we can stay at the top of the page, where you can easily see that in the **Package Files** section there are links to 32-bit and 64-bit Windows systems. For Linux users, even if there is an option here to download PuTTY, you probably want to read more and find that you have already installed a program that does this job.

After downloading PuTTY, it is important to know that you do not need to install this software, just open it, and the UI should appear on the screen. You will see the following screenshot:

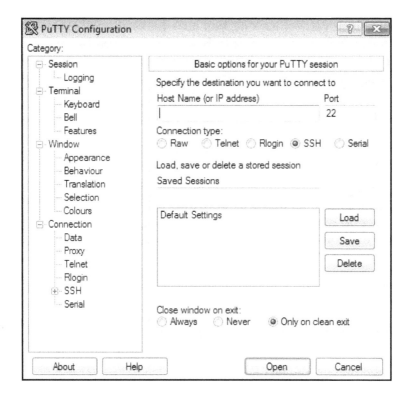

The next step is to define the hostname of the IP address of your remote server. Since, in this project we will be connecting the client to the Raspberry Pi Zero W server, we have to find the Pi's IP address; for example, going through your router's interface, you should find the IP. After this, you have to insert it in the Host Name (or IP address) field similar to the following image. My Raspberry Pi has the IP address `192.168.1.125`:

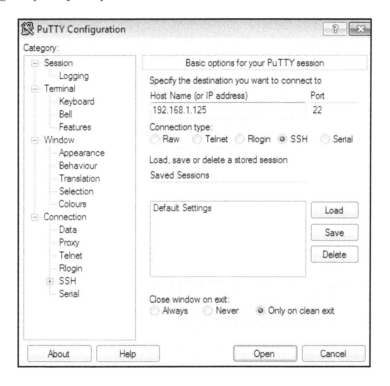

By clicking on **Open**, you should see a message saying something about the fingerprint. Everyone that creates an SSH connection leaves a fingerprint on the Raspberry Pi Zero W server, so since you are a new client, you just have to click on **Yes**; for example, a possible fingerprint should be as follows:

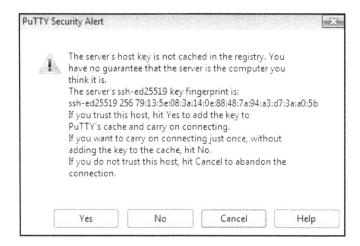

After this, you will be prompted to insert your remote server username and password. After inserting the username, as you can see in the following image, you will be prompted to set the password field. Note that by typing the password, there will be no characters inserted in the `putty` terminal, so type it slow and correct. In the following screenshot, we typed username as `pi` and default password as `raspberry`:

Keep in mind that after connecting to the Raspberry Pi Zero W, you can change your password with the following command:

```
sudo passwd
```

Linux

Linux users do not have to download software; they can open a Terminal window and do the job there. The following guide will use Linux Mint but all the Debian-based distros should be similar. Hopefully, Mac users should not have to do anything different since they also have a terminal. The following details should cover all Linux users.

As mentioned previously, we will work through a terminal, so open up your terminal or console window, and type the following command:

```
ssh
```

You will see something similar to the following if you have installed ssh in your system (or it was installed by the system):

```
mark@zeus ~ $ ssh
usage: ssh [-1246AaCfGgKkMNnqsTtVvXxYy] [-b bind_address] [-c cipher_spec]
           [-D [bind_address:]port] [-E log_file] [-e escape_char]
           [-F configfile] [-I pkcs11] [-i identity_file] [-L address]
           [-l login_name] [-m mac_spec] [-O ctl_cmd] [-o option] [-p port]
           [-Q query_option] [-R address] [-S ctl_path] [-W host:port]
           [-w local_tun[:remote_tun]] [user@]hostname [command]
```

After you have found the Raspberry Pi Zero W IP address, you should create the following command and type it on your terminal, where the user is pi and ipaddr is the IPv4 address of your Raspberry Pi Zero W board:

```
ssh user@ipaddr
```

For example, in the following screenshot, we will connect to `192.168.1.125`:

```
mark@zeus ~ $ ssh pi@192.168.1.125

The programs included with the Debian GNU/Linux system are free software;
the exact distribution terms for each program are described in the
individual files in /usr/share/doc/*/copyright.

Debian GNU/Linux comes with ABSOLUTELY NO WARRANTY, to the extent
permitted by applicable law.
Last login: Tue Jun 27 16:27:48 2017 from 192.168.1.117
pi@raspberrypi:~$ _
```

Keep in mind that in the preceding screenshot, the system did not request a password. This is because the login exchanges some keys in the background but we will talk about this in a later section. In your case, you should be prompted to insert your password, and after this, if you hit enter, you should be against the Raspberry Pi bash. So, that is all.

Automating the SSH procedure

In the preceding example, typing the password every single time was necessary. Next, we will use rsa-keygen to auto log into your server. The idea is that we will create a unique key. Then, we will transfer it to the server, and every time we connect to the server via ssh, we will provide our key automatically, which will obviously match. This way we can connect without passwords and it is more secure. So, let's go step by step and see how we can automate this procedure:

1. Open up your terminal on the client side.
2. The first step is to create the key pair in the client. You can do this by typing the following command in the terminal:

```
ssh-keygen -t rsa
```

- Next, you will need to insert a file name. As seen next, you can type whatever you want here as the filename of your rsa key:

```
mark@zeus ~ $ ssh-keygen -t rsa
Generating public/private rsa key pair.
Enter file in which to save the key (/home/mark/.ssh/id_rsa): myrsa
```

3. The next step is to create a password. You can leave it blank, and just hit *Enter*. After this, hit *Enter* again. You should see something similar to the following, where the rsa keygen is created:

```
mark@zeus ~ $ ssh-keygen -t rsa
Generating public/private rsa key pair.
Enter file in which to save the key (/home/mark/.ssh/id_rsa): myrsa
Enter passphrase (empty for no passphrase):
Enter same passphrase again:
Your identification has been saved in myrsa.
Your public key has been saved in myrsa.pub.
The key fingerprint is:
SHA256:HsYau9pX8GlXpvKM8GR06kw/tUK/nFwZREEpc+Uq9u4 mark@zeus
The key's randomart image is:
+---[RSA 2048]----+
|              .+=|
|             o.+ |
|             +.. |
|        .. . +.  |
|      . S+ +o+.. |
|       *..@.+o. o|
|      o .@ O o.o.|
|       . .. = *+oo|
|       ..o.   +E. |
+----[SHA256]-----+
mark@zeus ~ $
```

4. Without closing the terminal or changing the current directory, you can find the files created by simply executing the ls command. In the preceding example, where we define the rsa key name as myrsa, there are two files generated. The first one is called myrsa, and the second one is called myrsa.pub. At this point, it is very important to understand that the file called myrsa (without the pub extension) is your PRIVATE key and is ONLY for you. You must never publish or send it over to anyone. It is just like your secret password.

5. Now, you need to transfer the myrsa.pub file to the remote host. More precisely, you need to place it in the ~/.ssh/ folder of the remote server.

6. The final step is to create (if it doesn't exist) the ~/.ssh/authorized_keys file, and copy whatever the myrsa.pub file contains to the authorized_keys file.

Now, you should be ready to log in without a password.

You can finally automate the ssh command with the following simple script file. Replace the IP address of the script with your own Raspberry Pi IP address:

```
#!/bin/bash
# This script opens an ssh connection with the Raspberry Pi
ssh pi@192.168.1.125
```

Save this script with the name cpi and place it in /bin in your Linux local machine. Now, the way that I love connecting with my Raspberry Pi Zero W is to simply press *Ctrl + Alt + T* to open up a Terminal and then, type cpi and hit *Enter*. Within three seconds, you are connected to the Raspberry Pi.

SFTP

SSH is great and you may already have used it to connect to your Raspberry Pi. However, sometimes, we need to transfer files from and to the Raspberry Pi board. SSH is not capable of doing that. We need to use another protocol to transfer our files easily and without making this procedure look hard. Again, depending on your operating system, you can use different software. Next, we will mention two ways of doing this; a way using UI that will work for Windows and Linux operating systems and one more way through the Terminal.

FileZilla

FileZilla is free software that you can easily download for Windows and Linux operating systems. You can download this from `https://filezilla-project.org/download.php`.

After downloading and installing FileZilla, you only have to define a few parameters:

- `Host`: Here, you need to place the host name or IP address of your Raspberry Pi Zero W board
- `Username`: Define the username. Usually, it is `pi`
- `Password`: Define the password here. The default password is `raspberry`
- `Port`: The port number is `22`

The FileZilla interface has four main sections, as follows:

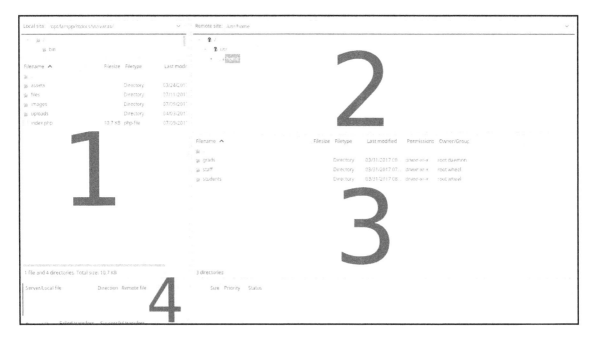

In the first section, you have your local machine files. In the second section, you have the folders of your remote server (Raspberry Pi), and in the third section, you have the files in the selected folder from the second section. Lastly, in the fourth section, you have the status of the transferred files. While transferring, you will see that all the files are in a queue and some of them are successfully transferred, while others have failed. In a successful file transfer, obviously, we need all the files to be transferred successfully.

Terminal

It is well known that everything you can do using software with UI can be done using a Terminal. Apart from the `ssh` command, there is one more that allows us to transfer files. Type the following command in your terminal:

```
sftp
```

Similar to the ssh manual, you will see something similar to the following; the syntax is pretty much the same:

```
mark@zeus ~ $ sftp
usage: sftp [-1246aCfpqrv] [-B buffer_size] [-b batchfile] [-c cipher]
            [-D sftp_server_path] [-F ssh_config] [-i identity_file] [-l limit]
            [-o ssh_option] [-P port] [-R num_requests] [-S program]
            [-s subsystem | sftp_server] host
       sftp [user@]host[:file ...]
       sftp [user@]host[:dir[/]]
       sftp -b batchfile [user@]host
mark@zeus ~ $ _
```

So, to connect to a server with the purpose of transferring files, we need to execute the sftp command as follows:

```
sftp user@IPaddr
```

Here, the user is our username on the remote server. In the Raspberry Pi, it is `pi` and the `IPaddr` is the IP address of the Raspberry Pi. In our example, it is `192.168.1.125`. If we execute this command, we will see that it needs our password. Using the preceding procedure that we have already described, we can automate the needed password. However, after submitting the password, we will see that the bash has changed. Now, there are two ways to interact with the remote server. We can `put` and `get` files from the server. You can easily transfer files from the remote server to your local machine with the get command:

```
get file1.txt
```

Alternatively, you can upload files from your local machine to the remote server using the `put` command:

```
put mylocalfile.txt
```

Note that depending on the local machine directory from which we started the `sftp` command, we can put and get files accordingly. This means that if we were in the `/home/nick/ folder`, we can directly upload only files that are inside in the nick folder with the put command.

 For more information about `ssh` and `sftp`, read the manual page with:

- `man ssh`
- `man sftp`

Networking

Setting up your website is one thing. Setting up all the scripts, rules, and networking parameters that will allow you to access the website all over the world is another and very important thing. In this section, we will discuss how you can access your router to define and set up some rules so that your website can be accessed from everyone. Also, we will discuss some things about your dynamic home IP address, define a problem that you may face and how you can solve it. Lastly, we will have an introduction to security layers that will be discussed in more detail in the next chapter.

By now, you should have access to your website locally. To sum up all the previous chapters, here is a step-by-step guide showing what you should have performed. It is important to have a look back before reading the Networking section, where we will perform some actions relevant to the router and the local network.

1. Download or create your website files.
2. Use FileZilla to transfer website files to the Raspberry Pi.
3. Install the XAMPP package on the Raspberry Pi.
4. Create a new folder under `/opt/lampp/htdocs/` with the name `mywebsite`.
5. Move all the websites into `/opt/lampp/htdocs/mywebsite`.
6. Verify from your mobile phone or any other computer in your local network that the `<raspberrypi-IP>/mywebsite` URL is valid and it displays your website.

Router access

Now, to gain access to your router, you have to find your router's IP address. It is usually 192.168.1.1, but depending on your mode, it may be different. If you are having trouble, you can check your router's manual and find out exactly what you have to do. Also, you can make a call to your ISP and ask them. Assuming that you found your router's IP address, now you have to open a browser and type the following URL:

```
http://192.168.1.1/
```

Alternatively, you can enter your router's IP address if it is different. Note that sometimes we need to specify the port number. To do this, we need to type the port number apart from the IP address to make a request from 192.168.1.1 in port 8080, as follows:

```
http://192.168.1.1:8080
```

You should see something similar to the following screenshot:

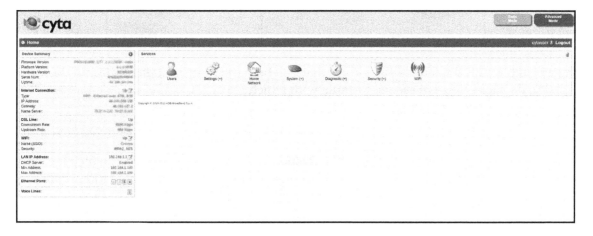

This is the interface of your router and here, you can change many things.

Port forwarding

First, let's understand why port forwarding is important and then, we will go through a way of setting this up. Without port forwarding, there is no way that our router would possibly determine the host target of an incoming connection. In other words, when you create a connection with a home router from your mobile phone, you do not know the IP of your Raspberry Pi. Now, let's see the general idea behind port forwarding. In the following screenshot, you can see that we have a router with IP 20.1.1.1 and we have two devices: a desktop computer and a laptop:

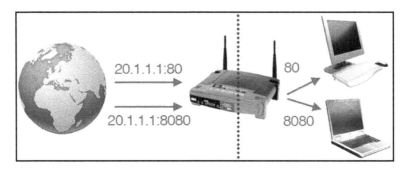

As a result, we need to create some rules that will help the router to determine and decide what to do. Here, you can see the formula with which we create a rule. Let's denote the following command as INC:

```
{<incoming connection IP>, <incoming connection port>}
```

Now, let's do the same with Raspberry Pi. Raspberry Pi is now a web server, which means that it handles requests in port 80 as HTTP protocol indicates. So, we denote RPI as follows:

```
{<raspberry pi IP>, <80>}
```

At this point, the only thing that we have to do is to create a rule, as follows:

```
INC -> RPI
```

With this, we actually mean that we direct every incoming connection from any IP at the port <incoming connection port> to <raspberry pi IP> in port 80. To sum up, your port forwarding rules should look as follows:

Traffic Coming from	External Port		Internal Port
Any Host PPP - Ethernet over ATM, 8/35	TCP 2880	⇨	6869
Any Host PPP - Ethernet over ATM, 8/35	TCP 22	⇨	Same Port
Any Host PPP - Ethernet over ATM, 8/35	TCP 4545	⇨	80

Depending on your router manual, there are many different ways to access your port forwarding settings or port mapping settings. To find out, read your router manual. In the preceding image, for any incoming connection on port 2880, go to the 6869 port at a specific IP address that I have not displayed for security reasons.

Home IP address

Before saying anything about IP addresses, it is important to know how the internet works, how the networks are connected to each other, and what exactly is going on. Assuming that every home has a router, each home has an IP address that is not static thus, it is changing without alerting you. In your local network, all your IP addresses have the same network part and a different host part. This means that if your local network is 192.168.1.X, the three blocks are the same for all your devices, including your router and the last one marked as X differs according to the device. Usually, the router has X = 1, your first connected device has X = 2, and so on. However, this is not a rule and it is not guaranteed. Your home (or router) may have an IP, such as 46.34.6.23, which must be used to retrieve messages and data from the internet servers. What happens now is each time you send a package from your computer to IP 192.168.1.125 on the internet, your router is responsible for changing the IP address 192.168.1.125 to the home IP 46.34.6.23.

When it comes back, it changes 46.34.6.23 again with IP 192.168.1.125. This procedure is called **NAT,** which stands for **Network Address Translation**. The following image shows an example of NAT:

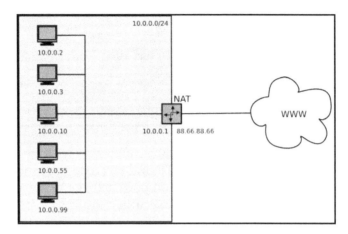

In the preceding image, all the IPs that start with 10.0.0.X are hosts and the routers have local IP 10.0.0.1. and external IP 88.66.88.66. The problem here is that your home IP address changes because your contract with your ISP provider has a dynamic IP address. Either you have to change it to a static IP address or you have to find a way of knowing your home IP address. Of course, since static IP addresses are not unlimited, you have to pay some extra money, so if your budget is big enough, go for this solution. As a result, you only have to find your home IP address once and it will not change. For all the others that do not want to pay, there are not many things you can do. A solution that I have figured out is to simply write a Python code that creates a connection to a server. This server can be free or paid (in case you own one). At this point, your server knows your home IP address. So, what you have to do is simply request your home address from your server.

Security layers

To create an introduction to the next chapter, we will mention some things about the security of our system; things that you should do and things that you shouldn't do. Setting up your router to port forward connections is something that you should keep in mind. It is not exactly a security hole but you should not disable any firewalls for sure. Each router has a firewall to protect you and your whole local network from unauthorized users. Your ISP has a firewall too and obviously, your computer has a firewall. You can disable all of them and let your computer free on the internet, however, this is way too risky. So, the first security layer that you should keep in mind is firewalls and whether it is wise or not to disable them.

It is important to know that only a firewall will know if an incoming connection will be harmful or not. A firewall is something that checks every incoming connection, and depending on your configuration, it allows or blocks the connections. Sometimes, especially when we are playing games, this is annoying because for some reason, the connection relevant to the game is blocked and we are kicked out. So, people simply disable almost everything.

The next security layer that we will talk about falls under the question: From whom you want to be secured? We all know that the world is not safe, thus the whole internet is quite dangerous. No one can possibly say, OK now I am 100% secure. There is no such thing. So, the question is from whom you want to be secured. There are some layers here. First, you may want to be secured from your family. This requires you to simply create passwords and often this is enough. The next layer is to be secure from your friends. Obviously, this is about creating passwords but you also have to keep some things to yourself; for example, you do not want to publish your home IP address or the port that you are working on. The first step of an attack is called *gathering information,* so the less the attacker knows about your network setup, the better.

Security

In every system, the final matter is security. Obviously, making your website and your connection secure is not a simple thing to do. It requires knowledge, and in this section, we will discuss the basic concept of security. We will also mention some actions that you should take to prevent unauthorized users accessing your files.

Router Interface

First of all, let's start from the settings in your router interface. These settings may differ according to your router model but eventually, you will have more or less the same as I have. Usually, all the ISPs provide low-cost routers with a basic configuration. In the following image, you can see that we have some options in the security tab of the router:

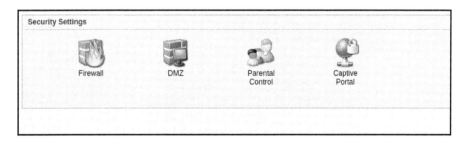

Next, let's see what each of these options do:

- **Firewall**: The first option is a firewall. Here, we can activate or deactivate and set the security level. If for some reason your application doesn't work, it is advised to enable a low-security level rather than disabling it entirely.

- **DMZ**: DMZ stands for Demilitarized Zone. DMZ is a physical or logical subnetwork that separates an internal local area network (LAN) from other non-trusted networks, such as the internet. In this security setting, you have to specify the external interface, such as PPP - Ethernet over ATM, 8/35 (IP-Address) and the internal IP address.

- **Parental Control**: This setting is used mostly for home security, for your kids, your parents, and similar situations. The basic idea of parental control is that a parent defines which websites all the other users can visit and which are marked in the black list. The following image shows exactly what options we have in this security setting:

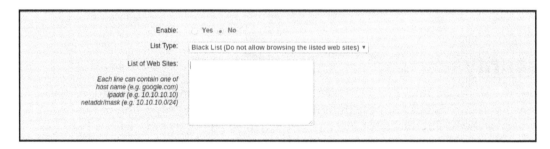

1. **Captive Portal**: Captive Portal is a web page that is displayed to new users before gaining access to the internet. It is usually used to display a paying option, check-in in a bar, or stuff like this. In the following image, we can see some settings relevant to the captive portal:

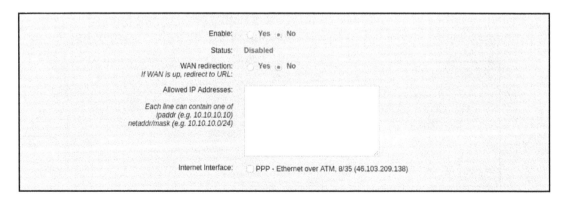

Computer

As far as the computer is concerned, there are two or three settings that we must perform. First of all, since we are talking about the Raspberry Pi Zero W board, the default password is `raspberry`, so obviously you need to change that to something more secure with letters, numbers, and symbols.

We can do this with the `passwd` command. Using a terminal, type:

```
passwd
```

You will be prompted to insert your current password. After this, you have to insert the new password twice. Now, if you exit and log in again, your password must have changed. Note that changing your password requires further actions if any kind of code or automation has been done in other script files.

ISP

As far as the **Internet Service Provider** (**ISP**) is concerned, there are some options that you can change. You have to call your ISP and request all the settings relevant to security that you can change. Feel free to ask and change all the settings as you want.

Summary

In this chapter, you learned about hosting and how you can set up your Raspberry Pi Zero W board to host a simple website. We went through some security issues that may come up while hosting a website and saw different ways to connect to your remote server Pi board. In the next chapter, we will go through all the steps to set up a home assistant. Home assistants are quite famous these days, allowing you to order things from Amazon, listen to your own music, and control your home.

9
AlexaPi

Previously, we went through a detailed project guide on how to set up and configure our Raspberry Pi Zero W board for hosting our personal website. We also talked about networking and looked at all the steps that we have to take to give access to our website to anyone in the world. In this chapter, we will go through a different project using AI and resources available on the internet to set up AlexaPi. AlexaPi is a clone project from the Alexa service by Amazon. Since Alexa is quite expensive, you can have a clone in your Raspberry Pi Zero W board costing the minimum amount of money. At the end of the chapter, we will mention some advantages and drawbacks of this project. In this chapter, we will talk about the following topics:

- Creating an Amazon developer account
- Setting up Raspberry Pi
- Installing Alexa
- Voice recognition
- Network administration

Creating an Amazon Developer account

Before downloading the necessary software, we have to create a new Amazon Developer's account so that we can access Amazon's Developer Services. Then, we will use **Amazon's Alexa Voice Services** (**AVS**) in our Raspberry Pi Zero W board for free. We have to download it from `https://github.com/`, then, install it on our Raspberry Pi Zero W board. After this, we will test it out to see how it works.

To create your personal account, if you do not have one, simply visit `https://developer.amazon.com/`, and click on the **Sign in** option in the top-right corner, and you will see the following screen:

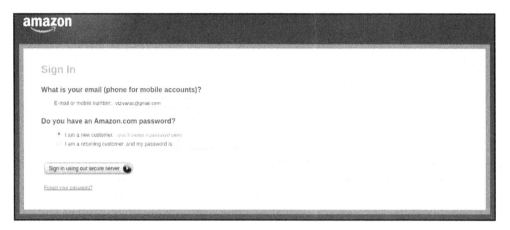

Here, you can sign in or register if you have no account. After this, verify the email from Amazon and sign into the Developer page. You should open the Developer dashboard page, that will look similar to the following page:

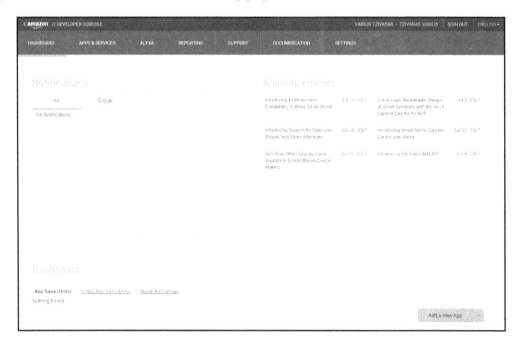

The next step is to navigate to the **ALEXA** tab, where you will see two options available. The first one is **Alexa Skills Kit**, and the second one is **Alexa Voice Service**. As discussed previously, we will use the second option here, called **Alexa Voice Service** or AVS. Click on the **Get Started** button, and let's create and set up all the necessary actions:

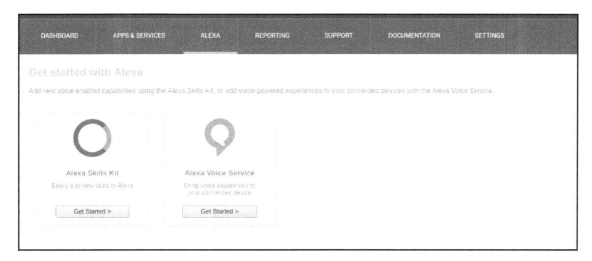

Alexa Voice Service will open a list of devices. In your case, if you have not performed this procedure before, you will probably have zero devices there. However, as you can see next, there is already one device, which we will ignore for the sake of simplicity:

Now, we have to click on the arrow on the **Register a Product** button, and select **Device**. Our Raspberry Pi Zero W will be the device that we register to AVS. After this, you should see the following image, where you are now prompted to fill in the required fields:

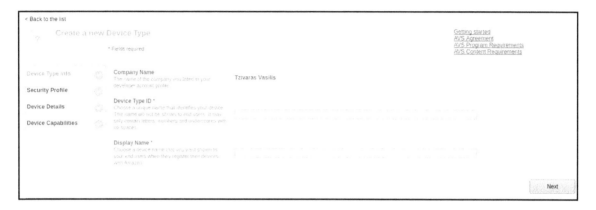

In **Device Type ID**, you have to specify a simple ID for your product. You can call it whatever you want. Furthermore, in the **Display Name** field, you have to specify the display name of the developer portal. Usually, **Device Type ID** is a name without spaces (you can use _), and **Display Name** is a field where you specify a name, so it is easier for you to understand and identify what it is. When you are ready, click on **Next**, and you will see the next section regarding the security profile, as follows:

In the **Security Profile** section, you have to select from the **Select Security Profile** drop-down menu, the profile of the device you are registering. It should have only one option. If not, create a new profile. Before you click on the **Next** button, more settings should appear in a horizontal menu.

In the **General** tab, as you can see in the following image, you have to specify **Security Profile Name** and **Security Profile Description**:

For example, you can set **Security Profile Name** as **Sample app security profile** and **Security Profile Description** as Alexa Voice example. After you have set these two options, click on **Next**, and you will see that there will be some IDs generated for you as follows:

Now, click on the **Web Settings** tab. Make sure that the security profile is selected in the drop-down menu, then, click on the **Edit** button on the right of the drop-down menu. After you click on the **Edit** button, you will be able to add another **Allowed Origins** and **Allowed Return URLs**:

In **Allowed Origins**, click on **Add Another** and type `https://localhost:3000`. Also, in `Allowed Return URLs`, click on the **Add Another** link, then type `https://localhost:3000/authresponse`. Now, we are ready to click on the **Next** button and proceed to the next section. In the following image, you can see that in **Device Details**, we can define how the device will look in the `init` screen that was mentioned at the start of the tutorial:

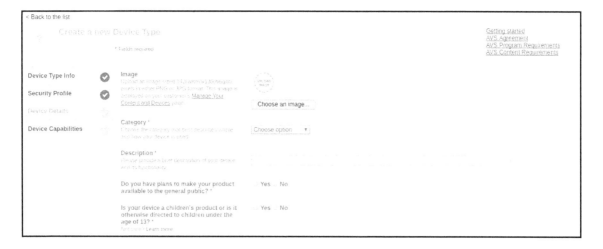

Here, you have to specify an image for your device. Google `Raspberry Pi`, and pick an image to place there. This should be enough. After this, in **Category**, select **Other** and, in the description, provide a simple description of your project, such as **Alexa service sample test**. Then, click on **Next**, and you will see that we are almost ready. The following page should appear, where you are prompted to view your settings and click on the **Submit** button:

As you can see in the following image, I have two devices there since I already had one, but you will see this one too:

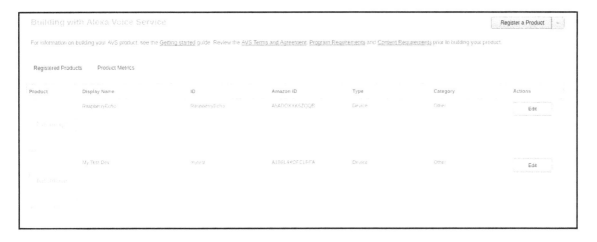

Now, we have to enable the security profile that we just created. To do this, we need to visit `https://developer.amazon.com/lwa/sp/overview.html` and select the **Security profile** that we created, then, click on the **Confirm** button. The following image shows the page, where you should activate your security profile:

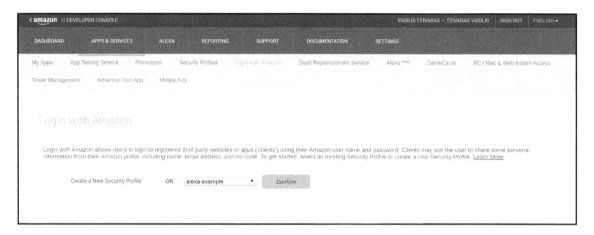

You need to enter a URL that begins with `http://` or `https://`, for example, `http://mytestexample.com`. After this, you can click on the **Save** button:

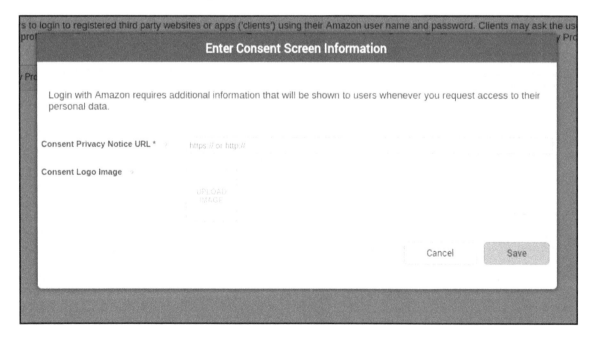

Next to the **Alexa Voice Service Sample App Security Profile**, you have to click on **Show Client ID** and **Client Secret**. As a result, you will see the client ID and client secret. You need to copy and paste them in a notepad because we will need those values later:

At this point, you have successfully created your Amazon's Developer account and it is ready.

Setting up Raspberry Pi

Before installing everything on our Raspberry Pi Zero W board, we need to download the latest distribution of Raspbian on our computer and use any kind of tool that works to install the software on our SD card. After this, we need to insert the SD card to the Raspberry Pi and power it on. We will use a GitHub repository for the next step. So, open up a terminal and type the following command:

```
git clone https://github.com/alexa/alexa-avs-sample-app.git
```

With the preceding command, you clone the repository `alexa-avs-sample-app` on your local computer. In this repository, you need to find the installation script and execute it, but before this, you need to make some changes. While creating our developer account and setting this up, we went through three important fields. So, we need to find `ProductID`, `ClientID`, and `ClientSecret`. After we have found these values, edit the `automated_install.sh` file using your favorite editor and change the appropriate fields. As a result, it should look like this:

```
ProductID="RaspMyExample"
ClientID="amzn.xxxxx.xxxxxxxxx"
ClientSecret="2662rge4xxxxxxxxxxxxxxxxxxxxxxxxxxxxxx6b4f9"
```

Next, you will need to run the script. This installation script will install all the dependencies. To run the script, you have to first open a terminal, and after navigating to the downloaded files, run the following command:

```
. automated_install.sh
```

Installing Alexa

Now, we need to open two different terminals and run some commands. In the first terminal, we will authorize our sample application with AVS. To do this, you can run the following command:

```
cd /alexa-avs-sample-app/samples
cd companionService && npm start
```

If you do not have npm installed, you can install it by running the following command:

```
sudo apt-get install npm
```

You can see tha,t after running these commands, the server will run on port 3000.

In a new terminal window and without closing the first one, we will run the sample app that communicates with AVS. To do this, first cd to the samples folder as before, and then, use the mvm command:

```
cd alexa-avs-sample-app/samples
cd javaclient && mvn exec:exec
```

At this point, you should see a pop-up message that says, **Please register your device by visiting the following URL in a web browser and following the instructions:** https://localhost:3000/provision/d340f23434343443h3h3h34h27. **Would you like to open the URL automatically in your default browser?**. You have to click on **Yes** and open it in your browser.

In your Chromium browser, you may experience some errors, but you can try solving them by clicking on **Go Advanced**, and proceeding with localhost (unsafe). Next, enter your credentials on Amazon's website and click on **Next**. Finally, you will be redirected to a web page that begins with `https://localhost:3000/authresponse`, and you need to check that, in the body of the web page, it says, **device tokens ready**. Return back to your application and click on **OK**.

There is one last thing that we need to do to make this work. Of course, if you do not want a *wake up* word to activate your system, you can skip this step. However, it is usually easier to say something, then say your command, then click on a button or something like that. Thus, you need to open a terminal window again, and you will use the Sensory wake ward engine, so type the following command:

```
cd alexa-avs-sample-app/samples
cd wakeWordAgent/src && ./wakeWordAgent -e sensory
```

Alternatively, type this to use `KITT.AI`'s wake word engine:

```
cd alexa-avs-sample-app/samples
cd wakeWordAgent/src && ./wakeWordAgent -e kitt_ai
```

At this point, you are ready to use `Alexa` and talk to it. You can activate the software by simply saying `Alexa`. Then, you can say, for example, "What time is it?"

Voice recognition

At this point, you have had an incredible experience talking to your Raspberry Pi and getting back some answers to your questions. This is not something that Raspberry Pi Zero W can do. As a result, it is important to clarify how this works. In the following figure, you can see that your Raspberry Pi Zero W board is on the left, and as soon as it is triggered with the word `Alexa`, it changes to `Listen mode`. In `Listen mode`, it hears everything you say, and when you stop talking, it processes that speech input and sends it back to Amazon's servers.

Now, these servers somehow find the answers using AI and some other technologies to send the response back to the Raspberry Pi Zero W. As a result, the Raspberry Pi sends the answer as output back to you in your Bluetooth speakers or headphones:

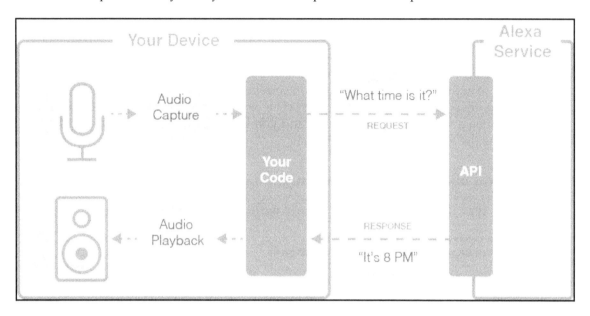

In the preceding image, you can see that the captured audio uses our Raspberry Pi Zero W code to make a request from the AVS API and get the response back. Once this is completed, the audio playback starts. You can understand that this procedure cannot be done in 1 second, so sometimes you have a delay of 4-5 or more seconds depending on your network and your location.

Official Alexa vs AlexaPi

Now, it is time to compare these two technologies. In this chapter, we developed a clone of "Alexa" over our Raspberry Pi Zero W. Obviously, both technologies are great and produce so many functionalities that the benefits outweigh the total cost. However, the official Alexa is quite expensive compared to a Raspberry Pi Zero W. So, in this, all the points go to Raspberry. Furthermore, AlexaPi is quite small compared to the official Alexa. Once more, the points go to Raspberry Pi. However, Raspberry Pi Zero W will not replace the official Alexa, and this is because it is a low-cost device that simply works. This project works better with the Raspberry Pi 3, since it has more hardware and it is easier to set up, but even with that the official Alexa was built exactly for this purpose. It probably has a longer working lifetime and minimum bugs that you can find in such a system.

To conclude, in my opinion, if you want to set up your home and buy more smart Amazon's things, go and buy Alexa and build your system like this. However, if you have a small budget, or you just want to test this out and play a bit, go for a Raspberry Pi board.

Network administration

We have seen how we can set up our Raspberry Pi Zero W board and add all of Alexa's functionalities. Now, we will discuss how you can take this project further and use the network in your home to control it. You can find in Amazon store many smart things, such as lamps that you can register in your Amazon Developer account and access them through your AVS. In the following image, you can see a smart lamp from Philips that is able to listen to your Alexa and take actions according to your AVS.

In the following image, you can see a smart lock system that is also capable of talking to your Alexa or any other device that you might have, and opening or closing a door for you:

These devices are only two of the hundreds of devices that the Amazon store has. You can find more devices by visiting the Amazon store and searching for Alexa. All these devices communicate over the network and, obviously, sometimes you need to control them from a long distance.

You can use the UBI application for Android users, since Amazon has not yet released an application for Android. For IoS users, you can simply download Amazon's application.

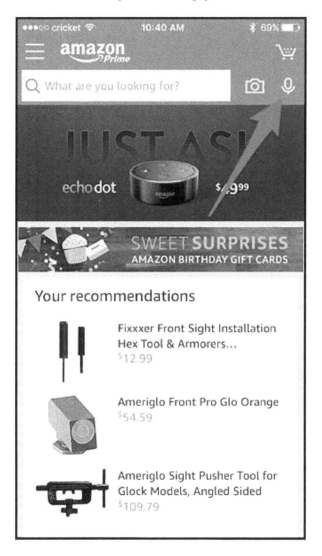

In the top-right corner, you will find a microphone. If you tap on this icon, you will see that you have some options. Click on the **Allow microphone access** button, as you can see in the following image:

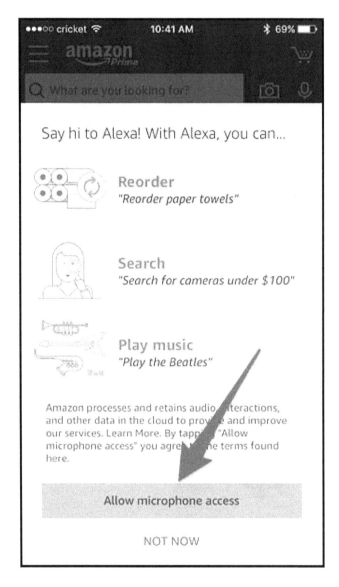

Then, allow all permissions that are necessary for that action, as you can see in the following image:

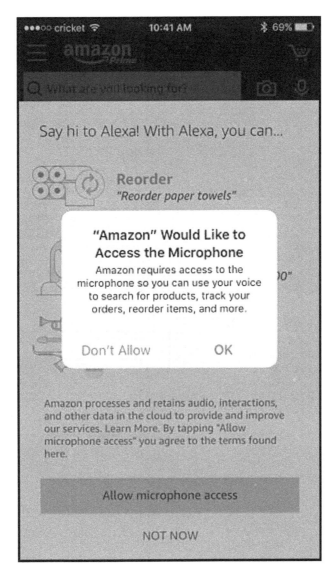

Lastly, you can talk to your Alexa even when you are not home. Through Wi-Fi networks and the internet, you can be connected to your Alexa from anywhere in the world.

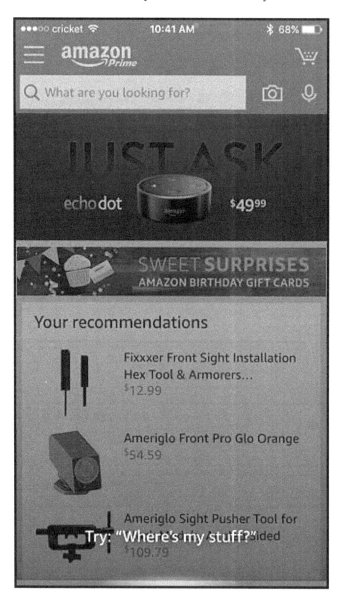

Summary

In this chapter, we have seen a simple way of setting up Alexa on your Raspberry Pi Zero W board. Even if Raspberry Pi Zero W does not have such capabilities, with the help of Amazon's server, we developed a system that listens to you and responds to your questions. In the next chapter, which will be the last one, we will build a weather station directly with the Raspberry Pi Zero W board using market components and show that Raspberry Pi Zero W's capabilities are endless.

10
WeatherPi

In the previous chapter, we have seen how we can install **Alexa** on our new Raspberry Pi Zero W board. Alexa is an awesome assistant, but Raspberry Pi Zero W's capabilities are higher. In this chapter, we will set up a weather station with our Raspberry Pi Zero W board. It will be able to transmit wireless data and connect to other devices that you might have, expanding your smart home with one more wireless project. We will use **Sense HAT**, which is commonly used in many projects. We will cover the following topics in this chapter:

- The Sense HAT module
- Set up a weather station
- Initial State
- Startup

The Sense HAT module

Sense HAT is an add-on board for Raspberry Pi 2 and 3, but it works with Raspberry Pi Zero as well. It was made especially for the Astro Pi mission.

The Sense HAT module looks as follows:

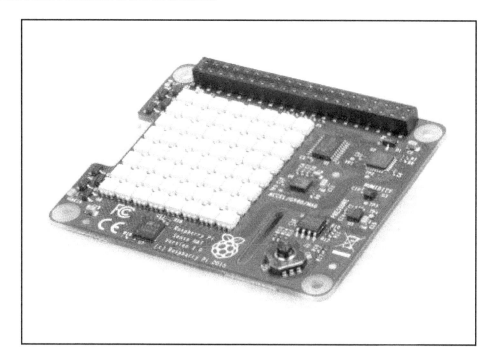

You can buy this from the official website, `https://www.raspberrypi.org/products/sense-hat/`. Sense HAT allows Pi to sense the world around it. With Sense HAT, we can display messages and images, control the orientation, gather sensor data, and respond to movement. As a result, Sense HAT is the easiest way of adding a ton of sensors to your Raspberry Pi Zero W board without buying and connecting jumpers to the breadboard. Sense HAT has the following functionalities:

- Orientation (yaw, pitch, and roll) via an accelerometer, 3D gyroscope, and magnetometer
- Temperature
- Humidity
- Pressure

It is also equipped with an 8x8 LED matrix that allows you to display data via various sensors. Through the LED matrix, you can also find which way geomagnetic North is by programming a compass using the magnetometer, or you can play games such as the old classic Tetris. Furthermore, you can use the joystick to enable a human user to interact with the programs on your Raspberry Pi board. As you will see in this chapter, writing programs for Sense HAT is quite simple using a Python library. Now, the following are some technical details about this module:

- **Gyroscope**: Angular rate sensor (dps) - ~245/500/2000
- **Accelerometer**: Linear acceleration sensor (g) - ~2/4/8/16
- **Magnetometer:** Magnetic sensor (gauss) - ~4/8/12/16
- **Barometer**: 260 - 1260 hPa absolute range (accuracy depends on the temperature and pressure, ~0.1 hPa under normal conditions)
- **Temperature sensor**: Accurate to ~2°C in the 0-65°C range
- **Relative humidity sensor**: Accurate to ~4.5% in the 20-80%rH range, accurate to ~0.5°C in 15-40°C range
- 8x8 LED matrix display
- Small five button joystick
- Stands may come in plastic or metal varieties

Weather station

Before you get started, you have to connect the Sense HAT module with your Raspberry Pi Zero W. Usually, Raspberry Pi Zero and Zero W come with non-soldered pins, so, if you haven't changed anything and haven't installed anything else, you will probably have to solder a GPIO pin extension to which you can install your Sense HAT easily. It is really up to you to set up this module, depending on your project and your hardware.

To start, let's update our Raspberry Pi Zero W board with the latest programs and updates. In the Raspberry Pi Zero and Zero W board, there are some issues, and updates are necessary. First, run the following command to update your Raspberry with the latest packages:

```
sudo apt-get update
```

Now, run the following command to upgrade your operating system to the latest one:

```
sudo apt-get upgrade
```

Now, run the following command to reduce as much as possible the chance of bugs and later errors:

```
sudo rpi-update
```

Next, add the following line to the end of the `/boot/config.txt` file:

```
core_freq=250
```

You can edit the file with a vim or nano editor. After this, you should be fine. So, let's continue to install all the necessary libraries and do the full setup. The next step here is to install the Sense HAT software package so that we can interact with the module. To do this, simply run:

```
sudo apt-get install sense-hat
```

Now, it is important to reboot your system. You can do this with the following command:

```
sudo reboot
```

Once you are back to your Raspberry Pi Zero W, you have to ensure that everything went OK and that your module has been installed correctly. To do this, we will write a simple program. Create the `sensehat_test` file with your favorite editor (for example, using vim):

```
sudo vim ~/sensehat_test.py
```

Now, we need to include the necessary libraries. First, from the `sense_hat` library, we need to include the Sense HAT module that allows us to interact with the Sense HAT module. To do this, we add the first line of code:

```
from sense_hat import SenseHat
```

The next step is to create a link to the library, and therefore we initialize a `variable` that will allow us to interact with further calls to this library. Do this with the following command:

```
sense = SenseHat()
```

Lastly, with the following command, you will see `"Hello World"` in the Sense HAT LEDs. We can write a message directly to the Sense HAT:

```
sense.show_message("Hello World")
```

Now, save and quit your file. To run your script, you must simply execute the following command:

```
sudo python ~/sensehat_test.py
```

At this point, as we said previously, you should see the text `"Hello world"` appear on the Sense HAT module. If not, try to replace the pins and fit them properly into your Raspberry Pi Zero W pinout. If you get errors, try resetting your Raspberry Pi and executing that Python script again. Next, you can find the full code to test this out:

```
from sense_hat import SenseHat
sense = SenseHat()
sense.show_message("Hello World")
```

At this point, Sense HAT should be ready and we can now go to step two, where we will install and configure the weather station. Create a new file with your favorite editor:

```
sudo vim ~/weather_script.py
```

Now, start writing some code. First of all, as we do in every Python script, we need to import all the necessary libraries. We can do this with the following lines of code:

```
#!/usr/bin/python
 from sense_hat import SenseHat
 import time
 import sys
```

The `sense_hat` library is necessary to interact with Sense HAT. We need this library because we will read from the sensors. The `Time` library from Python standard libraries is necessary because we can use it to do many things with time, such as add a delay. Lastly, the `sys` library allows us to access variables and functions that are usually managed by the interpreter. As we said previously, the first line that we see in the next block of code initializes Sense HAT, so we can perform further calls to the functions relevant to the Sense HAT module:

```
sense = SenseHat()
```

The following line clears the LED matrix in the Sense HAT module so we can have a clear matrix to write the results:

```
sense.clear()
```

In this block of code, we will create a `while` loop that will run forever and will stop if *Ctrl+C* is pressed. We can do this with Python using Indent, where it needs with the following block of code:

```
try:
        while True:
```

The next step is to get the temperature from the Sense HAT library. We can get this with one line of code using the library that we imported in the beginning. Notice that the output is in Celsius, so if you want to convert it to Fahrenheit, you have to make the conversion yourself:

```
temp = sense.get_temperature()
```

Now, you may need to convert the temperature to the closest decimal number. You can do this using the following code:

```
round(temp, 1)
```

So, to sum up, if you want the temperature expressed in Celsius, then you have to execute the following command:

```
temp = round(temp, 1)
```

On the other hand, if you want the temperature expressed in Fahrenheit, you have to run the following command:

```
temp = 1.8 * round(temp, 1)  + 32
```

The last line of the code that we will write is to print the value of the temperature. In case you want to print the Celsius temperature, type the following command:

```
print("Temperature C",temp)
```

You can also replace the C with an F if you have previously converted the temperature to Fahrenheit. Apart from the temperature, we will get the humidity and pressure values from Sense HAT. Sense HAT provides these values just like the temperature, so it is pretty much the same lines of code:

```
humidity = sense.get_humidity()
humidity = round(humidity, 1)
print("Humidity :",humidity)

pressure = sense.get_pressure()
pressure = round(pressure, 1)
print("Pressure:",pressure)
```

The last line of code uses the time library. We need to sleep the code execution for one second so that we can see the flow of data. We will do this with the following code:

```
time.sleep(1)
```

When `KeyboardInterrupt` is triggered, we ignore the exception, so we can have the script leave the `while` loop running. We will do this with the following code:

```
except KeyboardInterrupt:
 pass
```

Without the preceding lines of code, when the user pressed *Ctrl+C*, the program would end. The following is the full code:

```
#!/usr/bin/python
 from sense_hat import SenseHat
 import time
 import sys

 sense = SenseHat()
 sense.clear()

 try:
      while True:
           temp = sense.get_temperature()
           temp = round(temp, 1)
           print("Temperature C",temp)

           humidity = sense.get_humidity()
           humidity = round(humidity, 1)
           print("Humidity :",humidity)

           pressure = sense.get_pressure()
           pressure = round(pressure, 1)
           print("Pressure:",pressure)

           time.sleep(1)
 except KeyboardInterrupt:
      pass
```

Save and exit from the editor with the file name as `weather_script.py`. Next, run the Python script:

```
python weather_script.py
```

Now, you should see the temperature, humidity, and pressure on your screen, for example:

```
('Temperature C', 30.0)
 ('Humidity :', 39.8)
 ('Pressure:', 1025.7)
```

At this point, if everything goes well, you should be able to see these values on your screen. If you want to change the way they appear, you can always go back to your Python script file to edit the way they are printed. In the following section, we will display these values in a cooler way.

Changing the Python script we have written and displaying the data to the LED matrix in Sense HAT is not a big deal. There is already a call to Sense HAT, where you can print a string to the matrix. So, what we have to do is simply concatenate all the data we want to pass to Sense HAT in one string. The first step is to edit the file that we created before. Do this with vim or any other editor you like; for example, using vim, we can do this with the following code:

```
sudo vim weather_script.py
```

Next, we use the command that puts your program to sleep for one second:

```
time.sleep(1)
```

We need to add a new line of code. This new line of code combines all the data from the sensor that we get at the start of the program and displays them in one line in Sense HAT:

```
sense.show_message("Temperature C" + str(temp) + "Humidity:" +
str(humidity) + "Pressure:" + str(pressure), scroll_speed=(0.08),
back_colour= [0,0,200])
```

It is important to write the previous command in one line of code. In the sense, we display a message. The message is the concatenation of " " strings such as "Temperature C" and str() that is integer numbers converted into strings with the str() command from the Python library. The scroll speed is set to 0.08, but we can change it to more or less. Depending on the way the text was changed, the color was set to blue. Next, we need to make a call to the sense clear with the following code:

```
sense.clear().
```

This way, we will ensure that the LED matrix is completely cleared if we end the script for any reason. The full code is displayed as follows:

```
#!/usr/bin/python
from sense_hat import SenseHat
import time
import sys

sense = SenseHat()
sense.clear()

try:
    while True:
        temp = sense.get_temperature()
        temp = round(temp, 1)
        print("Temperature C",temp)

        humidity = sense.get_humidity()
        humidity = round(humidity, 1)
        print("Humidity :",humidity)

        pressure = sense.get_pressure()
        pressure = round(pressure, 1)
        print("Pressure:",pressure)

        sense.show_message("Temperature C" + str(temp) + "Humidity:" +
str(humidity) + "Pressure:" + str(pressure), scroll_speed=(0.08),
back_colour= [0,0,200])

        time.sleep(1)
except KeyboardInterrupt:
    pass

sense.clear()
```

Now, save and exit the file that you were editing. Run the script again with the following code:

```
sudo python weather_script.py
```

Now, you should see the text scroll across the Sense HAT LED matrix area. You will notice that there is one problem here. You cannot display all the data at once. This can be handled with an external monitor or the next section of the chapter. Now, you will see how you can improve your Raspberry Pi weather station with Initial State.

Initial State

We will continue the building of the weather station with Initial State, a website that acts as data storage and data analysis for IoT projects using Arduino, Raspberry Pi, and similar. There are other services like Initial State as well, but not all of them support Sense HAT. The first step here is to create an account with Initial State; I will explain everything in the following images. Visit `https://www.initialstate.com/`, and sign up for your account. The following image is the **INITIAL STATE** website page. Click on the **SIGN IN** link in the top-right corner:

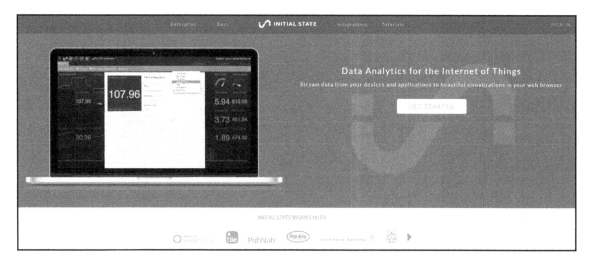

Click on the register link and fill out the registration form that you can see next with your **Email** and **Password**. You can also request a two-step verification using your mobile phone number. It is a good practice to add another security layer to your account:

Account Registration

Email   Sign Into An Existing Account

youremail@gmail.com

Password   8+ letters or numbers

••••••••••••

Repeat Password   An Anti-Typo Technology™

••••••••••••

Subscription Code   if you have one

e.g., Abc123 (case-sensitive)

✔ Use two-factor authentication to sign in

SMS-Capable Phone Number

📱   +30   69485156··

✔ Stay signed in   Register

Registering implies agreement to the Terms of Use.

When you fill out the form, you can click on the **Stay signed in** option to log in automatically. You will be redirected to the dashboard, which should look similar to the following image:

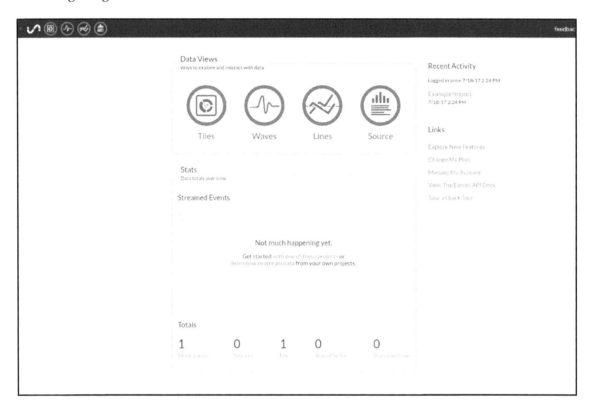

Next, click on the email address in the top-right corner and scroll to the bottom of the page, where you can find an option that allows you to create a new key. The button should look as follows:

Click on **Create A New Key**, and then write down the key that was generated. Now, go back to your Raspberry Pi Zero W board and open the terminal window. We now need to install the Initial State Python streamer. Before executing the command to grab the Initial State, you can verify the website with `https://get.initialstate.com/python`.

Then, you can simply run the following code:

```
curl -sSL https://get.initialstate.com/python -o - | sudo bash
```

To get data from Initial State to your Raspberry Pi Zero W via SSH deny the download of the example code, and, after the installation is complete, go and edit your weather station file. You can do this with the following code:

```
sudo vim weather_script.py
```

The previous code should be inserted below the line:

```
import sys
```

Add the following line of code that will include the Initial State streamer package to your script:

```
from ISStreamer.Streamer import Streamer
```

Now, we can use this package to set up your Python script and connect it to the Initial State API before the line:

```
sense = SenseHat()
```

Add the following line of code so that you can create the streamer and initialize the connection. You have to replace YOUR_KEY_HERE with the appropriate key that you received at the bottom of the Initial State website before:

```
logger = Streamer(bucket_name="Sense Hat Sensor Data",
access_key="YOUR_KEY_HERE")
```

Next, go through all of your code and find all your instances of:

```
print(
```

All instances of print should be replaced with the following code:

```
logger.log(
```

This change means that you print messages and information to the Initial State server and not your screen. Finally, your code should look as follows:

```python
#!/usr/bin/python
from sense_hat import SenseHat
import time
import sys
from ISStreamer.Streamer import Streamer

sense = SenseHat()
logger = Streamer(bucket_name="Sense Hat Sensor Data",
access_key="YOUR_KEY_HERE")
sense.clear()

try:
      while True:
            temp = sense.get_temperature()
            temp = round(temp, 1)
            logger.log("Temperature C",temp)

            humidity = sense.get_humidity()
            humidity = round(humidity, 1)
            logger.log("Humidity :",humidity)

            pressure = sense.get_pressure()
            pressure = round(pressure, 1)
            logger.log("Pressure:",pressure)

            time.sleep(1)
except KeyboardInterrupt:
      pass
```

Once you have done this, save and exit the file and run your new script file with the following code:

```
python weather_script.py
```

The new code will directly send the data back to the Initial State server. If you get any errors, check your internet connection. Now, go back to the Initial State website and open the dashboard. You can see the new data at the top-left side. Select your data and then click on **Tiles** to view an awesome graph of your data.

The data is now visualized, as shown in the following image:

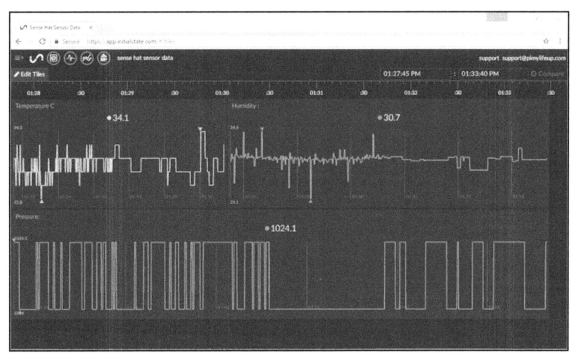

Startup

At this point, your WeatherPi Station should be ready. There is one more thing to do here. We can set our Python script to start when the Raspberry Pi Zero W board is booting. To do this, we need to install a package named `dos2unix` that actually converts DOS style line endings into something that is Unix friendly. Apart from this, you can use `crontab` (install it if you don't have it) or edit your `/etc/init.d/` to add some lines and make your script start with the other Raspberry Pi Zero W built-in services. To install the package mentioned previously, we have to run the following code:

```
sudo apt-get install dos2unix
```

Next, we have to set up our Python script as a service, so we can start it at the Raspberry Pi Zero W boot. To do this, we will create a new script that will allow us to start/stop it and handle the Python script as we want. As always, open your favorite editor and start creating a new script. We will use vim as our editor:

```
sudo vim /etc/init.d/weatherstation
```

It is time to write some code here. Start by writing the following code:

```bash
#!/bin/bash
### BEGIN INIT INFO
# Provides:          weatherstation
# Required-Start:
# Required-Stop:
# Default-Start:     2 3 4 5
# Default-Stop:      0 1 6
# Short-Description: Start/stops the weatherstation
# Description:       Start/stops the weatherstation
### END INIT INFO

DIR=/home/pi
DAEMON=$DIR/weather_script.py
DAEMON_NAME=weatherstation

DAEMON_USER=root

PIDFILE=/var/run/$DAEMON_NAME.pid

. /lib/lsb/init-functions

do_start () {
    log_daemon_msg "Starting system $DAEMON_NAME daemon"
    start-stop-daemon --start --background --pidfile $PIDFILE --make-
pidfile --user $DAEMON_USER --chuid $DAEMON_USER --startas $DAEMON
    log_end_msg $?
}
do_stop () {
    log_daemon_msg "Stopping system $DAEMON_NAME daemon"
    start-stop-daemon --stop --pidfile $PIDFILE --retry 10
    log_end_msg $?
}

case "$1" in
    start|stop)
        do_${1}
        ;;
    restart|reload|force-reload)
        do_stop
```

```
            do_start
            ;;
      status)
            status_of_proc "$DAEMON_NAME" "$DAEMON" && exit 0 || exit $?
            ;;
      *)
            echo "Usage: /etc/init.d/$DAEMON_NAME {start|stop|restart|status}"
            exit 1
            ;;
   esac
   exit 0
```

After writing all this code to an editor, you can save the file and exit. To ensure that everything runs smoothly, you need to run `dos2unix` on the file that you just created. To do this, you need to run the following code:

```
sudo dos2unix /etc/init.d/weatherstation
```

With this command, you ensure that the file is written correctly and everything is OK. Now, you need to change the permissions in your Python script. If you don't do this, your bash script will fail to work. To do this and change your permissions, run the following command:

```
sudo chmod 755 /home/pi/weather_script.py
```

The next step is to modify and change the permissions of your weather station bash script. You have to give execution permissions, and you can easily do this with the `chmod` command:

```
sudo chmod +x /etc/init.d/weatherstation
```

Create a symbolic link between your bash script and the `rc.d` folders:

```
sudo update-rc.d weatherstation defaults
```

Now, start your Python script:

```
sudo service weatherstation start
```

At this point, you should be ready. Your weather station service should automatically start on boot. You can check this by rebooting your Raspberry Pi Zero W board. Furthermore, you can interact with your weather station with some more commands; for example, you can start a service with the following code:

```
sudo service weatherstation start
```

Alternatively, if, for any reason, you want to stop a running service, you can simply run the following command:

```
sudo service weather station stop
```

Now, there are two more commands to go. The next one actually kills the process and starts it again. So, to reload the weather station, just run the following command:

```
sudo service weatherstation reload
```

Finally, to get the current status of the weather station, run the following command:

```
sudo service weather station status
```

This way, you should be able to find whether it is running or it has stopped.

Summary

From this chapter, you should have learned how to create, set up, and improve your personal weather station using **Sense HAT**. There are several modules available to buy and add them to your project. Sense HAT provides us an opportunity to create this weather station, and since Raspberry Pi Zero W is so small, it can be used to make a portable weather station. Since this is the last chapter of the book, you have seen that there are many different modules that you can buy for your Raspberry Pi board to expand its capabilities, and, assuming that you can handle the wireless communication as you have been taught in this book, you can create wireless projects using just a $10 board. This is a great opportunity to develop skills and create useful projects that expand your knowledge.

Index

A

accessories, Raspberry Pi Zero W
  HDMI to mini HDMI cable 20
  HDMI to VGA cable 21
  micro SD card 20
  OTG cable 17
  PowerHub 18
  RCA jacks 22
Acoustic Playlist 148
advanced client-server communication
  advanced client 112
  advanced server 107, 112
AFMotor library
  reference 88
Alexa
  installing 192
Amazon Developer account
  creating 183, 186, 188, 190
Amazon's Alexa Voice Services (AVS)
  download link 183
Arduino microcontroller 75
audio 142

B

battery 85
Bluetooth sensor 82
breadboard 84

C

caching 161
camera
  installing 117
chat services
  about 57
  Chatfuel 57
  Converse 58

Facebook messenger 59
  Flow XO 58
  Google cleverbot 60
chatbot 49
Chatfuel 57
client-server communication
  about 101, 158
  client request 158
  communication protocols 159
  simple client 105
  simple server 102, 105
communication protocols
  about 32
  internet protocols 33
  IoT protocols 33
Converse 58

D

data
  secure transfer 61
DC motors 65, 73
dd tool
  reference 26
distributions
  about 23
  Raspbian distribution 25
distributors
  about 27
  reference 27
Domain Name Server (DNS) 157

E

encoder
  about 68, 70
  reference 74

F

face recognition 131, 135
Facebook messenger
  reference 59
FaceDetect
  reference 131
file transfer
  connecting for 43
FileZilla
  reference 43, 172
  used, for file transfer 43
Flow XO 58
four motor mobile robots 93, 96
FTP (File Transfer Protocol) 159

G

Google cleverbot
  about 60
  reference 60
GPIO header 19

H

hardware
  overview 70
HC06 82
home automation
  completing 113, 116
home bots 99
HTTP (Hyper Text Transfer Protocol) 159
Hyper Text Transfer Protocol Secure (HTTPS) 159

I

Initial State
  used, for building weather station 212, 216
Internet of Things (IoT) 31
Internet Protocols (IP) 32
Internet Service Provider (ISP) 37, 181
IoT protocols
  6LowPan 35
  about 33
  bluetooth 34
  LoRaWAN 35
  near field communication (NFC) 35
  Wi-Fi 35

Z-Wave 34
Zigbee 34

L

legacy tokens
  reference 108

M

market speakers
  about 137
  reference 138
microcontroller
  creating 89
  developing 89
  programming 88
mobile robot, components
  Arduino microcontroller 75
  battery 85
  bluetooth 82
  breadboard 84
  DC motor and wheels 73
  encoder 74
  Motorshield 77
  others 86
  servo 78
  ultrasonic sensor 79
mobile robot
  about 63
  future versions 92
mood selection system, adding
  about 148
  code 150
  hardware 149
MotionPie settings
  configuring 122
  file storage 126
  general settings 123
  motion detection 128
  motion movies 128
  motion notifications 129
  still images 128
  Text Overlay 126
  video device 124
  video streaming 126
  wireless network 124

Working Schedule 129
MotionPie
  camera outside of local network, connecting 121
  installing 120
  multiple network cameras, setting up 121
motor
  soldering 86
Motorshield 77
music files
  about 142
  online music services 143
  security 143
music speakers
  software setup 139, 140
MusicBox
  AirPlay streaming 142
  autoplay URL 141
  device name 141
  DLNA/uPnP/OpenHome streaming 142
  root password 142
  wait time 142

N

Network Address Translation (NAT) 37, 178
network administration 195, 200
networking settings
  network name 141
  SSD 141
  Wi-Fi password 141
  workgroup 141
networking
  about 174
  router access 175

O

official Alexa
  versus AlexaPi 194
OpenCV
  installing 130
  reference 131
OTG cable 17

P

Pi Music Box
  reference 139

PowerHub 18
proxy servers 161
PuTTY 42

R

Raspberry Pi 2 model
  specifications 9
Raspberry Pi 3 Model B
  about 15
  specifications 13
Raspberry Pi 3 model
  specifications 8
Raspberry Pi 5MP 1080P Camera NoIR
  reference 118
Raspberry Pi 5MP Camera Board Module
  reference 118
Raspberry Pi Zero board
  specifications 10
Raspberry Pi Zero W
  about 7, 12
  accessories 16
  automatic authentication 42
  camera support 16
  card adapter 20
  case 22
  case protection 29
  connecting 36
  connecting, for command execution 41
  connecting, to Internet 39
  debugging, steps 28
  GPIO header 19
  internet 36
  issues 28
  local network 37
  microSD card issue 29
  music, playing 146
  network administration 40
  NOOBS distribution 24
  port forwarding 39
  securing 45
  securing, with firewall 46
Raspberry Pi
  about 7, 8
  reference 12
  setting up 191

Raspbian distribution
  reference 25
RCA jacks 22
remote control
  about 164
robotics
  fundamentals 63
Rock Playlist 148
router access
  about 175
  home IP address 177
  port forwarding 176
  security layers 178

S

SCP
  used, for file transfer 45
Search Engine Optimization (SEO) 156
security tab options, router interface
  Captive Portal 180
  DMZ 180
  Firewall 180
  Parental Control 180
  parental control 180
security
  about 179
  computer setting 181
  Internet Service Provider (ISP) 181
  router interface, using 179
Sense HAT module
  about 11, 203
  reference 204
  technical details 205
server response 160
servo mechanism 78
SFTP
  about 171
  Filezilla 172
  terminal 173
slack
  reference 107
socket programming
  about 100
  advanced client-server communication 107
  simple client-server communication 101

sound players
  about 143
  Alsamixer 144
speaker
  connecting 145
SSH clients
  Linux 169
  Windows 165
SSH
  about 164, 165
  clients 165
  procedure, automating 170

T

torque 66

U

ultrasonic sensor 79
user input
  about 49
  chatbot development 54, 57
  server installation 50, 52

V

voice recognition 193

W

weather station
  about 205, 207, 211
  building, with Initial State 212, 216
  startup 217
web hosting
  about 153
  definition 154
  domain name 156
  services 155
  setup 157
website development
  about 162
  local access, allowing 164
  XAMPP/LAMPP, using 163
wheel 67, 68

Wide Area Network (WAN) 35
WideRaspberry Pi Zero W
    setup 36

X

XAMPP
    download link 163

www.ingramcontent.com/pod-product-compliance
Lightning Source LLC
Chambersburg PA
CBHW080638060326
40690CB00021B/4989